Project Transformation®

Transforming Communities Through Relationships

intern
guidebook

created by the

MISSIONAL WISDOM FOUNDATION

Original artwork and layout by Wendi Bernau
Original content by Stephanie Evelyn McKellar, Wendi Bernau, and Katey Rudd

Published by Missional Wisdom Foundation
www.missionalwisdom.com

for use by Project Transformation
www.projecttransformation.org

guidebook at a glance

Each week includes:

living in balance
mind, body, spirit

thoughts on vocation

muévete
devotionals

liturgy

scriptures

going deeper resources

friday experience
reflection prompts

journaling pages

Project Transformation®
Transforming Communities Through Relationsh

You are an integral part of Project Transformation's legacy! We believe transformation happens through relationships, where all teach and all learn. We are grateful for your leadership and learning and for your unique perspective. We invite you to bring your whole self and add your voice to this ministry. We also invite you to lean into your peers and your leaders for support.

Project Transformation started as an idea sketched on a paper napkin and grew into a movement led by enthusiastic young adults and innovative churches with a ton of faith and grit. What started 20 years ago in Dallas, Texas, is now a national ministry partnering with over 40 host churches in nine United Methodist Annual Conferences in dozens of cities with 400 young adults leading more than 3,500 children and youth!

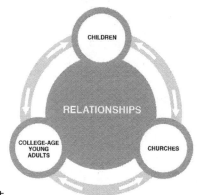

Welcome to the family, where our mission includes three Cs: to engage **College-aged young adults** in purposeful leadership and ministry, support **Children** in holistic development and connect **Churches** to communities. You will learn more about Project Transformation's mission and values and how they shape our ministry in this guidebook.

Our prayer is that your experience will **empower you to explore and live out your vocation** through identity formation, intentional community, servant leadership, and spiritual disciplines. Vocation comes from the Latin word *vocare* which means "to call." Vocation is finding the unique voice God has given you. At Project Transformation, vocation is understood as a journey of discovering your authentic self and how God invites you to make your greatest contribution. This life-long journey neither begins nor ends here. However, we hope your experience will support continued discovery of your voice and God-given vocation.

Individual reflection without action and a posture of responsibility, love, and justice in Christian community is empty. Service and leadership without spiritual reflection is void of greater lasting significance. So, we encourage you to utilize this guidebook to fully engage the young adult experience— from community dinners, to muévete, to worship, to individual prayer and reflection, to Friday Experience—since these elements work in concert toward the larger goal of vocational discernment in community.

Blessings upon your summer journey. May these pages bear witness to a living God at work in your life, the growth you experience, and your thoughts and thanksgivings. Who knows? Like an idea sketched on a paper napkin, your notes may birth a beautiful, faithful movement.

Peace be with you,

Project Transformation Staff

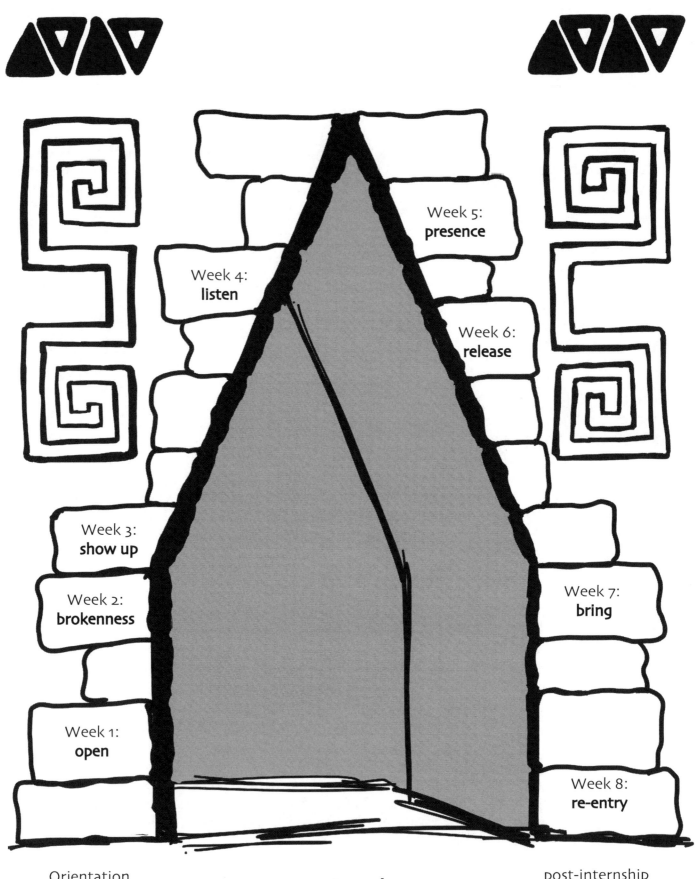

Week 5:
presence

Week 4:
listen

Week 6:
release

Week 3:
show up

Week 7:
bring

Week 2:
brokenness

Week 1:
open

Week 8:
re-entry

Orientation

enter in

post-internship
and next steps

orientation

- **living in balance:**
  mind, body, spirit
  primary and secondary foods
  rhythms of work and rest

- **discovery:**
  identity formation
  spiritual awareness
  intentional community
  servant leadership

- **exploration:**
  vocational discernment
  inspiration

- **liturgy:**
  the work of the people
  being part of a larger community

- **friday experiences:**
  reflections on calling
  assessing community needs

why use this book?

elements of the intern experience

daily rhythms:
muévete (with the large group and on my own)
living in balance: mind, body, spirit (on my own)
journaling (optional)

weekly rhythms:
small group options (with others)
worship service (with the large group)
table liturgy and conversation (at community dinners)
friday experiences (on my own and with others)

 why muévete?

"Muévete" is the Spanish imperative, meaning "move yourself".
"Muévete" is a time to move and be moved
physically, emotionally, and spiritually.
It is a time to come together to begin the day in a focused, excited way.

The moniker for this morning space was given in honor of a beloved worship song in Spanish called "La Montaña" ("The Mountain"). This song is rooted in Matthew 17:20 (NRSV) which says:

"For truly I tell you, if you have faith the size of a mustard seed, you will say to this mountain, 'Move from here to there,' and it will move; and nothing will be impossible for you."

Perhaps playing this song for the first Muévete can help build an understanding of the singing and dancing and faith aspects of beginning the morning as such.

Tell those mountains to move it.

Monday through Thursday focuses on one of the four core areas of Project Transformation: Identity Formation, Intentional Community, Servant Leadership, and Spiritual Disciplines. A fifth day is for you to engage in rest and sabbath with your devotional time as an individual or in community with others. Use this anytime Friday through Sunday.

Begin each devotional by reading the Liturgy for the Week.

Scriptures are included each day.

Pages for journaling and processing the devotional questions are located at the end of each week throughout the book.

You may want to accompany the morning devotional with a spiritual practice.

why friday experiences?

While your experience with the children this summer will no doubt be impactful, your internship is primarily geared to invite your reflection on how you intersect with the world around you, especially when it comes to reflecting and discerning on vocation, and how you'd like to show up and offer your gifts to the world.

The Friday Experiences are meant for you, inviting you into snapshots of different emanations and expressions of ministry, compassion, advocacy, and justice in the world. Lean into these experiences, and listen deeply to what your soul and body tell you as you show up here. Allow these questions before and after to invite you into deeper reflection with yourself and among each other.

 why living in balance?

holistic wellness

Health is not simply the food you eat, drink you drink, and supplement you take. You could eat all the broccoli and kale you can afford each day and still experience anxiety, lack of passion and direction, loneliness, etc. Health is a matter of mind, body, spirit, and community.

In Integrative Nutrition we observe two kinds of foods: Primary & Secondary Foods

Primary Foods have four main food groups:

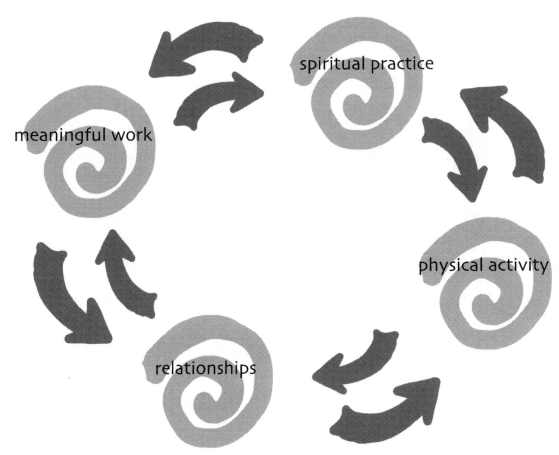

These are the four most important sources of nutrition for your mind, body, and spirit. Without getting sufficient amounts of these, your holistic health will be poor.

Secondary Foods: the actual food and drink you put in your body.

We will focus on enhancing our **Primary Food** nutrition over the following weeks as we learn to practice wellness in mind, body, and spirit. This will look like a brief prompt, an exercise, and reflection each week.

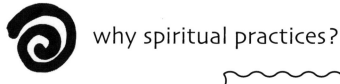 why spiritual practices?

spiritual practices

Good self care is essential.

We cannot pour out if we do not fill up.

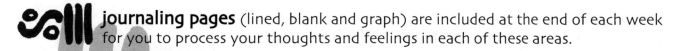

These nine weeks are going to stretch you physically, mentally, and emotionally. It is important to be able to find time for internal refreshment and renewal. The spiritual exercises outline some basic contemplative prayer practices or meditations that will help you cultivate internal awareness so that you can have a solid foundation from which to enter into the external areas of your life: work, relationships, and so on.

There is one practice per week. Each week, do that practice every day. Some will be familiar and some will be totally new to you. That's okay. Try everything and learn what works for you; discard what doesn't.

Pray as you can, not as you can't.

All the sections of this book are designed to engage your whole personhood.

Mind: reflection questions engage the mind and heart in thinking about life, faith, vocation, and social justice.

Body: Primary and secondary foods, nutrition, and exercise keep you energized and ready to go.

Spirit: Cultivating awareness and sensitivity connects us to our own interior life, to the Transcendant, and to the people around us (God, Self and Others).

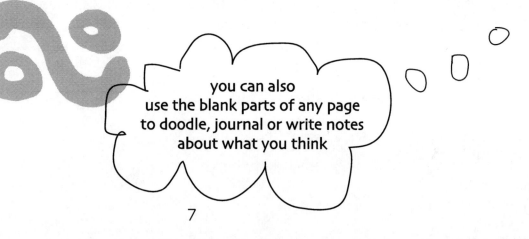 **journaling pages** (lined, blank and graph) are included at the end of each week for you to process your thoughts and feelings in each of these areas.

you can also
use the blank parts of any page
to doodle, journal or write notes
about what you think

 # why liturgy?

Liturgy ("the work of the people") connects the fibers and threads of our shared and distinct experiences to the active yet sometimes invisible and undetected presence of God. Liturgy connects us to other interns: across Project Transformation chapters as we walk parallel summer journeys, these shared words cultivate and shape culture and language to interpret our understanding of the work and God at work among us. Liturgy connects us to ourselves: the words weave themselves in and out of our journey as we return to them with daily rhythm and cadence. The words will bring new insight as our participation shapes and sharpens us, hitting us differently depending on the day and season.

While it may seem forced or inauthentic, Liturgy can serve as a discipline that sows seeds into our souls, rooting us within community and a resounding and anchored presence in God. Liturgy can provide hospitality for the moments we lack the words we need to express ourselves. Liturgy connects us to our history, tradition, and to those who have walked the journey of faith before us. Furthermore, Liturgy can empower us to create our own liturgies in our spaces and contexts, nurturing a powerful prayer practice of reflection and discovering the Spirit of God in all things. Liturgy invites us to pay attention, forming us as disciples with sacramental attention to the hidden and invisible movement of God among us.

 # why table liturgy and conversation?

The Table is the space where justice and friendship can happen across relationship, among mutuality, and through storytelling. Jesus used the practice of gathering at table to advocate for the humanity of others, to restore justice across divides, and to empower others to experience the presence of God among each other.

This section of Table Liturgy and Discussion questions is meant to nurture, equip, and sustain your reflection of the power and sacrament that is already at work each time you sit together at a table with others.

 # why going deeper resources?

There is a lot of fabulous work going on in the world, by lots of people—we'd love to introduce (or re-introduce) you to some of them.

Feel free to read the articles or watch the videos on your own or with a group anytime during or after your internship.

 table liturgy and conversation

the cycle of table conversation as we move through the eight weeks
from welcome (lower left) to create (lower right).
Notice how each week going in is echoed in the parallel week going out

week 4 justice (in conversation and story)
Seeing one another fully allows empathy and diversity to thrive. How is the table becoming a platform for story, dialogue, and listening? How is this space a place of equality?

week 5 invitation
You're invited to embody these revolutionary table qualities. Who else can be invited? Who is missing that could bring a new voice and perspective to this table space?

week 3 community (is forming)
How has this table space provided room for community to grow? The meal is a powerful place for relationships to build. How are you seeing one another more fully?

week 6 mutuality
There are different gifts around the table, can they all find a place here? How are you witnessing abundance as everyone brings their gifts and offerings?

week 2 hospitality
What in this experience makes you feel welcome and safe? What has made others feel welcome and safe? What stories are emerging from yourselves, others, and the food?

week 7 interruption
Hospitality invites interruption, allowing the space to be molded and shaped by all present and possibly present. What does it look like to invite the spirit and others to interrupt, change, alter, and co-create the space?

enter in

week 1 welcome (to the table)
May you arrive and feel welcome. Look around, who is present and who is not. What cultures and stories are here. What is the potential of this table space?

week 8 create
As you go from this space, how will you create other table (and meal) spaces of mutuality, justice, community, and relationship?

9

training week

preparation

training week: orientation
living in balance

 mind

The Wheel of Life

 body

The Wheel of Life is a metric for understanding your current health in twelve different categories of Primary Foods. Deeper understanding of what areas need more nutrition can help us prioritize goals for growth.

Instructions:

Begin by placing a dot in each pie slice rating your satisfaction level on a scale of zero to ten, with zero being NO satisfaction at the tip of the pie slice in the center of the circle and ten being COMPLETELY SATISFIED on the far outer edge of the pie slice
(Most of us will be somewhere in the middle for each)

Connect the dots once you have rated your satisfaction for each category.
This should give you an odd, multi-angled shape that reflects your current holistic wellness.

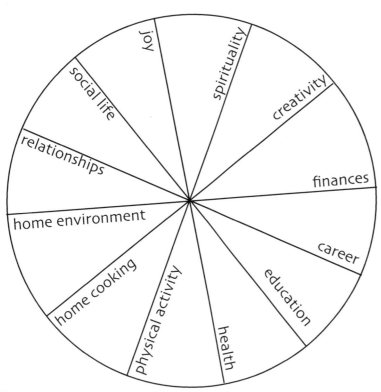

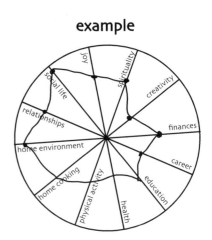

example

Reflection:

What do you notice about your current holistic wellness?

Where do you feel strong and satisfied?

What areas could use more nutritious input?

Were you surprised by anything? Share with your group.

spirit

 the practice of living in community

Rule of Life

A **Rule of Life** is like a personal mission/vision/values statement for yourself and/or your intentional community. What kind of person do you want to be? How will you interact with others? Take some time to consider the following questions:

- Prayers
  What will you do to develop your own spiritual life?

  What commitment will you make to learning and practicing spiritual disciplines?

- Presence
  How will you practice hospitality?

  How will you actively engage with the larger community?

- Gifts
  How will you practice generosity?

  How will you care for all of Creation?

- Service
  How will you engage in building community?

  What commitment will you make to find rest in the midst of this service?

- Witness
  How will you participate in social justice?

  How will you share God's presence with others?

Using your responses to these questions, sketch out a few ideas for your own Rule of Life

Write out your Rule of Life, decorate it, and post it in your space where you will be reminded of the commitments you are making to yourself and your community.

thoughts on vocation

**I BELIEVE
in knowing
WHO YOU ARE
but
WITHOUT LIMITING YOURSELF
to your own expectation of
WHO YOU ARE.**

-Charlotte Eriksson

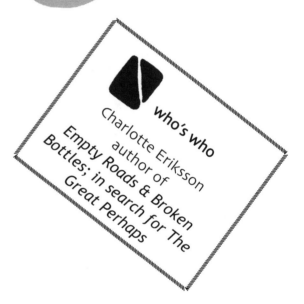

Here is where our **real selfhood**
is rooted,
in the divine spark or seed,
in the image of God
imprinted on the human soul.
The True Self is not our creation, but God's.
It is the self we are **in our depths.**
It is our capacity for divinity
and transcendence.

– Sue Monk Kidd

who's who
Charlotte Eriksson
author of
Empty Roads & Broken Bottles; in search for The Great Perhaps

liturgy of preparation

God, prepare us for the road that lies ahead
Prepare us in posture
Prepare us in practice
May we release perfection for the sake of being present
May we encounter you
in the wilderness
In work and in wonder
**Open us, shake us,
sift us and shape us**
Make us into the Imago Dei
Needed for what comes our way
**May we be present to our whole selves
mind, body, spirit, community**
Prepare the way
And us for it
Invite us, create us,
Lead us along road and into necessary rest
**That we might be those
Who know how to retreat and pray alongside you
That we might be those
Who know how to abide within you**
Prepare us, God,
For who
And how
And where
you are calling us to be

training week: orientation
monday: identity formation

 **scripture**

1 Corinthians 3:16
Don't you know that you are God's temple and God's Spirit lives in you?

1 John 3:1–2
1 See what kind of love the Father has given to us in that we should be called God's children, and that is what we are! Because the world didn't recognize him, it doesn't recognize us. 2 Dear friends, now we are God's children, and it hasn't yet appeared what we will be. We know that when he appears we will be like him because we'll see him as he is.

Genesis 1:27
God created humanity in God's own image, in the divine image God created them.

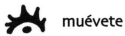 **muévete**

Devotional:

As you prepare for the summer, the internship, the children and youth, the work ahead, and all that is still unforeseen, each Monday will attend to what you are noticing within yourself. This day will invite you to listen to your heart and soul stirrings, your body in aches, pains, butterflies, and gut reactions, your brain as it processes, considers, articulates fears, analyzes, and reacts. Notice the narratives about who you are that you tell yourself and that others have told you.

What titles or identities do you claim?

Are there stories about yourself you would like to release?

Are there stories about yourself that you feel slipping away against your will?

In what ways do others name you?

How do you name yourself?

Each week Monday will focus on your own identity, how you craft it, where you receive it from others, how you claim it, and what God has to say about all of it. Each Monday will end with a prayer that shifts our attention to God in the presence of Creator; may this prayer help us notice what we discover within ourselves.

Creator God, whose image I bear, help me to pay attention to what is occurring within me.

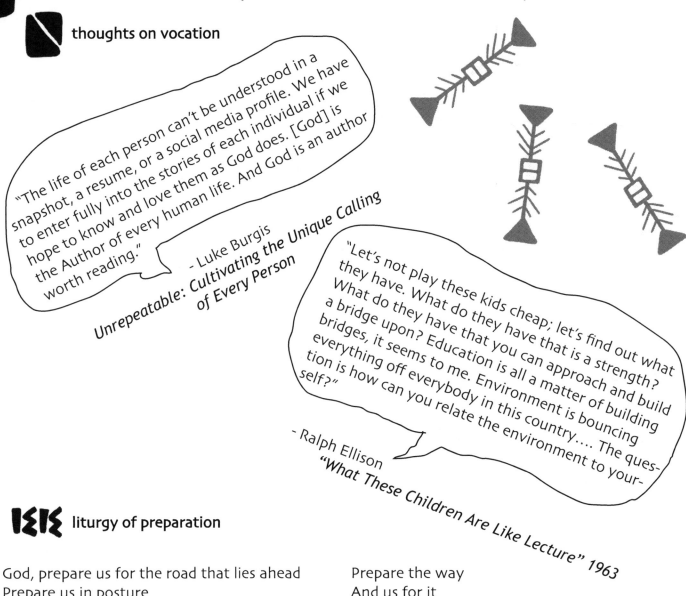

thoughts on vocation

"The life of each person can't be understood in a snapshot, a resume, or a social media profile. We have to enter fully into the stories of each individual if we hope to know and love them as God does. [God] is the Author of every human life. And God is an author worth reading."

– Luke Burgis
Unrepeatable: Cultivating the Unique Calling of Every Person

"Let's not play these kids cheap; let's find out what they have. What do they have that is a strength? What do they have that you can approach and build a bridge upon? Education is all a matter of building bridges, it seems to me. Environment is bouncing everything off everybody in this country.... The question is how can you relate the environment to yourself?"

– Ralph Ellison
"What These Children Are Like Lecture" 1963

liturgy of preparation

God, prepare us for the road that lies ahead
Prepare us in posture
Prepare us in practice
May we release perfection for the sake of being present
May we encounter you
in the wilderness
In work and in wonder
**Open us, shake us,
sift us, and shape us**
Make us into the Imago Dei
Needed for what comes our way
**May we be present to our whole selves
mind, body, spirit, community**

Prepare the way
And us for it
Invite us, create us,
Lead us along road and into necessary rest
**That we might be those
Who know how to retreat and pray alongside you
That we might be those
Who know how to abide within you**
Prepare us, God,
For who
And how
And where
you are calling us to be

 **scripture**

John 14:16–17
16 I will ask the Father, and he will send another Companion, who will be with you forever. 17 This Companion is the Spirit of Truth, whom the world can't receive because it neither sees him nor recognizes him. You know him, because he lives with you and will be with you.

Matthew 10:40
Those who receive you are also receiving me, and those who receive me are receiving the one who sent me.

 muévete

Devotional:
As you prepare for the lifestyle of the weeks ahead, the community and close quarters, the work and blessing and challenge of dwelling together in rhythm with a rule of life, each Tuesday will attend to what you are noticing within your intentional community. This day will invite you to hear the stories all around you, in those you like and dislike, in those who delight you and those who challenge you.

Who do you notice beside you?

Where do you notice God in the nearby and the neighbors?

In what ways will you be sharpened, shaped, and sensitive in the community in which you reside this summer?

Notice the stories told in the community beyond: who are these children, who are their families?

What expectations of themselves guide each of them or lack thereof?

How does the church define herself?

How is God showing up in the midst of the community and people around you?

This day each week will focus on the presence of God in the midst of community, relationship, interaction, and the messiness of humanity in all its forms. Each Tuesday will end with a prayer that shifts our attention to God in the Trinitarian presence; may this prayer help us notice God in diversity and interpersonal dynamic.

Community of Love dwelling in Parent, Son, and Holy Spirit, teach me to see your image in my brother, sister, enemy, friend, and neighbor.

training week: orientation
wednesday: servant leadership

thoughts on vocation

In other words, we may,
by fixing our *attention*
almost fiercely
on the facts actually before us,
force them to turn into *adventures;*
force them to give up their *meaning*
and fulfill their mysterious *purpose.*

— G.K. Chesterton

*Our strongest gifts
are usually those
we are barely aware of possessing.
They are a part
of our God-given nature,
with us
from the moment we drew first breath,
and we are no more conscious
of having them
than we are
of breathing.*

— Parker J. Palmer
*Let Your Life Speak: Listening
for the Voice of Vocation*

muévete

Devotional:

As you prepare for the work ahead this summer, for the ways you will give, pour out, even perhaps feel taken from, for the ways you will offer of yourself, support others, and show up to the tasks at hand, each Wednesday will attend to the gifts, capacities, and insights you bring and carry within you. This day will invite reflection on obvious and less apparent gifts, on abundance you may not have realized you possess, on skills and insights you have that others may lack, on offerings and assets that other spaces may need.

What do you see within yourself in the gifts of time, practices, knowledge, skills, talents, experiences that you can share with the community for the good of all?

What can you offer that nurtures those around you? What can you offer to your fellow humans?

What do you have that can bring light and life to situations around you this summer?

This day each week will focus on the ways and postures from which you can serve; you are invited to reflect on the many ways service can show up. The way you serve may not be the way others serve, and that is okay. Each Wednesday will end with a prayer that invites the serving posture of Jesus to be our guide into our gifts and out into the world around us.

Jesus, Servant of the Lord, empower us in the gifts we bring. Equip us to lead from where we are.

training week: orientation
wednesday: servant leadership

 **scripture**

John 13:12–17
12 When he had finished washing their feet, he put on his clothes and returned to his place. "Do you understand what I have done for you?" he asked them. 13 "You call me 'Teacher' and 'Lord,' and rightly so, for that is what I am. 14 Now that I, your Lord and Teacher, have washed your feet, you also should wash one another's feet. 15 I have set you an example that you should do as I have done for you. 16 Very truly I tell you, no servant is greater than his master, nor is a messenger greater than the one who sent him. 17 Now that you know these things, you will be blessed if you do them.

1 Corinthians 12:4–7
4 There are different spiritual gifts but the same Spirit; 5 and there are different ministries and the same Lord; 6 and there are different activities but the same God who produces all of them in every-one. 7 A demonstration of the Spirit is given to each person for the common good.

liturgy of preparation

God, prepare us for the road that lies ahead
Prepare us in posture
Prepare us in practice
May we release perfection for the sake of being present
May we encounter you
in the wilderness
In work and in wonder
**Open us, shake us,
sift us, and shape us**
Make us into the Imago Dei
Needed for what comes our way
**May we be present to our whole selves
mind, body, spirit, community**

Prepare the way
And us for it
Invite us, create us,
Lead us along road and into necessary rest
**That we might be those
Who know how to retreat and pray alongside you
That we might be those
Who know how to abide within you**
Prepare us, God,
For who
And how
And where
you are calling us to be

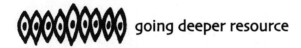 **going deeper resource**

Video: TED talk - Guy Winch "why we all need to practice emotional first aid"
What does it mean to practice emotional hygiene, taking care of our emotional and mental state with as much diligence and care as we do our bodies?

thoughts on vocation

"The two ideas, justice and vocation, are inseparable....
It is by way of the principle and practice of vocation
that sanctity and reverence enter into the human economy.
It was thus possible for traditional cultures
to conceive that 'to work is to pray.'"

- Wendell Berry

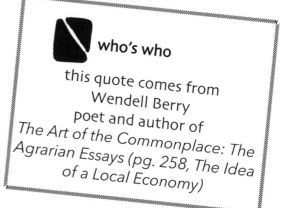

who's who

this quote comes from
Wendell Berry
poet and author of
The Art of the Commonplace: The Agrarian Essays (pg. 258, The Idea of a Local Economy)

 **muévete**

Devotional:

As you prepare for the rhythms, challenge, and weight of the internship experience ahead, what disciplines will you need to remain rooted within yourself and connected to life and community around you? What practices will serve you in the work and weariness, in the stillness and service, in the creativity and collaboration? What disciplines will make sure you are not forgotten as a person who is finite and in need of food, restoration, sleep, and play? What disciplines will make sure others are not forgotten as sharers of the space around you with their own needs and limits? What boundaries do you notice that are there to help you thrive and pause?

Take the wisdom you already know about yourself and what you need, and also be prepared to be surprised by what you need in this new experience. Even if you've done a Project Transformation summer before, each experience is its own unique thing. Pay attention to yourself and the scaffolding of disciplines that keeps you healthy and in harmony with God, yourself, and the world around you. Set a timer for ten minutes and write as a spiritual discipline, without stopping your hand or censoring yourself. What comes up for you as you read about these postures Jesus took?

This day each week will focus on some unconventional but crucial disciplines that will help nurture the work, and help nurture you and others in the process of the work. Dig deep, engage them and yourself with curiosity, notice how you show up and how they affect you. Each Thursday will end with a prayer that invites attention to the ways the Spirit moves within us, guides and directs us, and introduces us to ourselves through new rhythms.

Spirit of the Living God, may this discipline strengthen my spirit and equip me to dwell in love.

 scripture

Jesus...

...said No **Mark 1:35–38** Early in the morning, well before sunrise, Jesus rose and went to a deserted place where he could be alone in prayer.36 Simon and those with him tracked him down. 37 When they found him, they told him, "Everyone's looking for you!" 38 He replied, "Let's head in the other direction, to the nearby villages, so that I can preach there too. That's why I've come."

...slept **Mark 4:38** But Jesus was in the rear of the boat, sleeping on a pillow.

...entered wilderness **Luke 4: 1** Jesus returned from the Jordan River full of the Holy Spirit, and was led by the Spirit into the wilderness. 2 There he was tempted for forty days by the devil. He ate nothing during those days and afterward Jesus was starving.

...listened **Mark 5:33** The woman, full of fear and trembling, came forward. Knowing what had happened to her, she fell down in front of Jesus and told him the whole truth. 34 He responded, "Daughter, your faith has healed you; go in peace, healed from your disease."

...ate **Luke 24:41–43** Because they were wondering and questioning in the midst of their happiness, he said to them, "Do you have anything to eat?" 42 They gave him a piece of baked fish. 43 Taking it, he ate it in front of them.

...drank **Luke 7:33–44** John the Baptist came neither eating bread nor drinking wine, and you say, 'He has a demon.' 34 Yet the Human One came eating and drinking, and you say, 'Look, a glutton and a drunk, a friend of tax collectors and sinners.'

...asked for help **Mark 14:32–34** Jesus and his disciples came to a place called Gethsemane. Jesus said to them, "Sit here while I pray." 33 He took Peter, James, and John along with him. He began to feel despair and was anxious. 34 He said to them, "I'm very sad. It's as if I'm dying. Stay here and keep alert."

...asked questions **Luke 24:17–19** He said to them, "What are you talking about as you walk along?" They stopped, their faces downcast. 18 The one named Cleopas replied, "Are you the only visitor to Jerusalem who is unaware of the things that have taken place there over the last few days?"19 He said to them, "What things?"

...paused before answering **John 8:6** Jesus bent down and wrote on the ground with his finger.

...prayed **Luke 5:16** But Jesus would withdraw to deserted places for prayer.

...turned around **Mark 5:30** At that very moment, Jesus recognized that power had gone out from him. He turned around

...wept **John 11:35** Jesus began to cry.

...kicked over tables **Matthew 21:12** Then Jesus went into the temple and threw out all those who were selling and buying there. He pushed over the tables used for currency exchange and the chairs of those who sold doves.

training week: orientation
weekly check-in

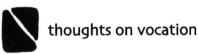 thoughts on vocation

"Once a seminary student asked to shadow me for two days to see what my life as a pastor was like.
At the end, he said,
"Oh my gosh,
you're basically a person for a living."

— Nadia Bolz-Weber

who's who

this quote comes from Nadia Bolz-Weber pastor and author of *Pastrix: The Cranky, Beautiful Faith of a Sinner & Saint*

 weekend check-in

No judgment, just noticing. How are you listening to your soul this week?

I was present and fully engaged in muévete ☐

I wrote out a Rule of Life ☐

I graphed my Wheel of Life ☐

I engaged in meaningful conversations with my community ☐

What do I want to remember from this week? (write it in this space)

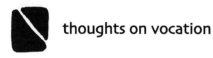

thoughts on vocation

OUR PRIMARY CALLING
in life
IS TO RECEIVE AND TRUST
this justice-making
and compassionate Love,
AND TO LIVE IT
into the world.

- CYNTHIA D MOE-LOBEDA

 scripture

Genesis 2:2b

...and on the seventh day God rested from all the work that God had done.

muévete

Devotional:

As you prepare for the road ahead and plan for all the teaching, games, discussions, events, activities, and relationships, be mindful of what you will need for restoration and rejuvenation of your body and soul. Try to embrace both the kind of rest that prepares you to return to the work, and also the leisure that allows you to accomplish nothing and still know your deep, inherent worth. You do not have to earn your worth.

You do not have to earn your worth, so how this summer will you practice being?

How will you practice slowing down, pause, and nothingness?

What will you need in order to embrace Sabbath? What may stand in the way of you slowing down and taking pause?

What feelings and memories do you associate with rest and doing nothing?

This day each week will focus on slowing down and paying attention, on pausing and releasing. God can be deeply known when we are at rest and still; our worth is not achieved by how much we accomplish. Each Fifth Day will end with a prayer that joins with the Psalmist, experiencing the guidance of the Good Shepherd leading us into rest and stillness.

Good Shepherd, lead me into rest. Lead me beside still waters. On this day, restore my soul.

training week: orientation
journaling pages

Liturgy of Openness

Oh Lord, let my soul rise up to meet you, **as the day rises to meet the sun.**
Open me up to this day, **that I might encounter you.**
In my own being, **may I encounter you.**
In my neighbor and community, **may I see your face.**
In the challenges and disappointments, **may I know your presence.**
In the celebrations and excitement, **may I share your joy.**
May we be open. May we be broken open. **May we see you in a new way.**

Prayers of the People

For the gifts within us waiting to be uncovered, discovered, and put to use...
...God, open our hearts and minds.

For the community we co-create here in this space, this home, this city, and this summer...
...God, equip us to be your body.

For the leadership we will be invited to practice...
For the ways our leadership and gifts will look different from each other's
For the insight to empower others to use their skills and gifts to lead...
...God, give us courage and compassion.

For the ways we will experience the presence of God, and for the moments we will yearn and find ourselves thirsty...
...God, be near to us in every moment.

For the children we encounter,
For the stories we hear,
For the brothers and sisters who share this community,
For our own story as we walk and discover who God is calling us to be,
...God, teach us how to honor our stories, the stories of others, and encounter your story throughout.

In your holy community of love, Creator, Son, and Holy Spirit, we pray, we participate, and we give thanks. Amen.

week

1

open

week 1: open
living in balance

 mind

 body

do it afraid

*Growing up, my father had a mantra that drove me nuts: **"Do it afraid."***

I would roll my eyes in resentment that he wasn't letting me off the hook for participating in an activity simply because I was fearful. Whether it was a piano recital, soccer tryouts, or giving a speech in class, his response was the same: "Ok. Do it afraid."

I value this lesson immeasurably now. We will be afraid, that's a given; **but we have control over how we use fear.** We can let it motivate us or limit us. We let fear get in the way of every single dream or goal when we settle for what is comfortable over what brings us to a new level. I alleviate my uncomfortable fear of failing at soccer tryouts easily: I don't go. I lose in the long run because I forfeit all the joy, growth, and community of being on the team.

Allowing fear to rule our actions keeps our lives small, closed, and safe. Greatness happens in the expanse of openness and risk, regardless of temporary discomfort, seeming failure, or who thinks we are being foolish. "Doing it afraid" can build nutrition **in each Primary Food: Spiritual Practice, Relationship, Meaningful Work, Physical Activity.**

Exercise week one: Do It Afraid

Do one thing this week that scares you. It could be rock climbing, singing in public, confronting someone who has wronged you, making a new friend, taking a dance class, seeking forgiveness, the sky's the limit. **SHARE WITH YOUR GROUP.**

Reflection:
Write about what you did that scared you this week. How did you feel before, during, and after?

Do you feel regret or accomplishment?

Do you feel more open?

week 1: open
living in balance

 spirit

the practice of being

Centering Prayer, much like meditation, teaches us to rest in God's presence. It is a practice of awareness and release, becoming aware of ourselves and those around us.

How do I arrive today? How is it with my soul?

The thoughts that arise while you are quiet will help you identify your innermost longings, fears, and concerns. Pay attention to them without judging them. Identify patterns. Be aware of how your mood affects your interactions with others. Ask God to help you sort through whatever comes up.

Let's try Breath Prayer:

Instructions:
Sit (or walk) quietly for fifteen minutes focusing only on breathing slowly and deeply in and out. Use your senses. Listen to the air moving. Smell a candle, herbs, or favorite blanket. Hold an object in your hand and feel the texture. Thoughts and associations will pop up. Notice them and let them float away like leaves on the surface of a river. Resist the urge to be productive and allow yourself be a human BE-ing instead of human DO-ing.

Tips: use a timer so you aren't worried about keeping track of time.

Contemplation isn't a quick fix. It might feel uncomfortable at first. Repetition and practice of still-ness and quiet brings long term benefits.

optional activity: drawing meditation
turn to a blank journal page and draw a line all the way across the very top of the page. Now add a series of close parallel lines until you have covered the whole page with lines (no rulers allowed). Notice how you feel as you are doing this. Are you judging yourself? Let go. Practice noticing what you are doing and how you are feeling as you move down the page without the added pressure of self judgment.

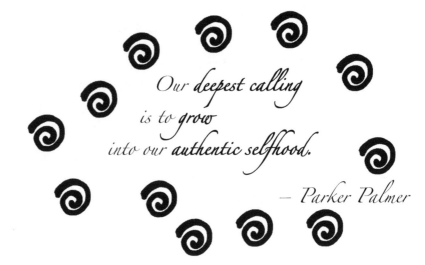

1

thoughts on vocation

Who am I?

Our deepest calling is to grow into our authentic selfhood.

— Parker Palmer

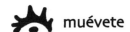 muévete

Devotional:

You have arrived to this work, this community, and this space. How are you feeling?

Pay attention to what you feel strong and weak in, what brings you passion, and what you avoid. You are discerning the unique and important way God has created you. You already know some of that. This summer experience will show you more of that.

Pay attention. What do you notice in your reactions and thoughts?

Where do you gravitate? What do you avoid?

The one who has begun a good work in you will bring it about to completion.

Creator God, whose image I bear, help me to pay attention to what is occurring within me.

week 1: open
monday: identity formation

 **scripture**

Psalm 139:5-7, 13–14

5 You surround me—front and back.
   You put your hand on me.
6 That kind of knowledge is too much for me;
   it's so high above me that I can't fathom it.
7 Where could I go to get away from your spirit?
   Where could I go to escape your presence?

13 You are the one who created my innermost parts;
   you knit me together while I was still in my mother's womb.
14 I give thanks to you that I was marvelously set apart.
   Your works are wonderful—I know that very well.

> Vocation
>   is a gradual revelation
>   of me to myself by God...
>   It is who we are,
>   trying to happen.
>   – James Whitehead

 **liturgy of openness**

Oh Lord, let my soul rise up to meet you, **as the day rises to meet the sun.**
Open me up to this day, **that I might encounter you.**
In my own being, **may I encounter you.**
In my neighbor and community, **may I see your face.**
In the challenges and disappointments, **may I know your presence.**
In the celebrations and excitement, **may I share your joy.**
May we be open. May we be broken open. **May we see you in a new way.**

week 1: open
tuesday: intentional community

thoughts on vocation

To open ourselves
TO THE TRUTH
and to bring ourselves
FACE TO FACE
with our personal and collective reality
IS NOT AN OPTION
that can be accepted or rejected.
IT IS AN UNDENIABLE REQUIREMENT
of all people and all societies
THAT SEEK TO HUMANIZE THEMSELVES
and to be free.

— Bishop Juan Gerardi

 liturgy of openness

Oh Lord, let my soul rise up to meet you, **as the day rises to meet the sun.**
Open me up to this day, **that I might encounter you.**
In my own being, **may I encounter you.**
In my neighbor and community, **may I see your face.**
In the challenges and disappointments, **may I know your presence.**
In the celebrations and excitement, **may I share your joy.**
May we be open. May we be broken open. **May we see you in a new way.**

muévete

Devotional:
Pay attention to the community around you, to the people in your home as well as in your work and community. Who are they? What stories, histories, and dreams do they bring? Community can be a means of grace, a way to show up to the presence and work of God. What gifts are here in this community?

Victor Hugo, the French poet and novelist, writes, "To love another person is to see the face of God." Pay attention to the ways God is revealed in the faces and stories and work of your neighbors and fellow human beings.

Community of Love, Parent, Son, and Holy Spirit, teach me to see your image in my brother, sister, enemy, friend, and neighbor.

week 1: open
tuesday: intentional community

 scripture

Exodus 33:12–14
Moses said to the Lord, "Look, you've been telling me, 'Lead these people forward.' But you haven't told me whom you will send with me. Yet you've assured me, 'I know you by name and think highly of you.' 13 Now if you do think highly of me, show me your ways so that I may know you and so that you may really approve of me. Remember too that this nation is your people."
14 The Lord replied, "I'll go myself, and I'll help you."

Who is in my community?

week 1: open
wednesday: servant leadership

thoughts on vocation

The secret of vocation **is to discover** *what it is you most* **truly and deeply want** *when you are most* **really and truly you.**

Fr. Michael Himes

 liturgy of openness

Oh Lord, let my soul rise up to meet you, **as the day rises to meet the sun.**
Open me up to this day, **that I might encounter you.**
In my own being, **may I encounter you.**
In my neighbor and community, **may I see your face.**
In the challenges and disappointments, **may I know your presence.**
In the celebrations and excitement, **may I share your joy.**
May we be open. May we be broken open. **May we see you in a new way.**

muévete

Devotional:
This work will demand much of you. You will find yourself tired and energized, nourished and sapped, sometimes all in the same day. Yet you have gifts and skills from which you can lead and serve. What are you seeing within yourself that you can offer? Who else do you know that models service and leadership?

Calling has been described by American writer and theologian Frederick Buechner as where "your deep gladness and the world's deep hunger meet." What do you imagine when you think of your deep gladness and joy as strengths? Think outside the box, begin from your own internal joy, hobbies, and talents. From there, imagine what it would look like to serve others and lead and work for justice from these places.

The world needs kind and just ministers, lawyers, doctors, writers, teachers, accountants, travelers, parents, astronauts, consultants, video game designers, and every other career endeavor. How are you being invited to lead and work for justice, to love God and love others, from exactly who God has made you to be?

Jesus, Servant of the Lord, empower us in the gifts we bring. Equip us to lead from where we are.

week 1: open
wednesday: servant leadership

 scripture

Philippians 2:1–10
Therefore, if there is any encouragement in Christ, any comfort in love, any sharing in the Spirit, any sympathy, 2 complete my joy by thinking the same way, having the same love, being united, and agreeing with each other. 3 Don't do anything for selfish purposes, but with humility think of others as better than yourselves. 4 Instead of each person watching out for their own good, watch out for what is better for others. 5 Adopt the attitude that was in Christ Jesus:
6 Though he was in the form of God,
   he did not consider being equal with God something to exploit.
7 But he emptied himself
   by taking the form of a slave
   and by becoming like human beings.
When he found himself in the form of a human,
   even death on a cross.
9 Therefore, God highly honored him
   and gave him a name above all names,
10   so that at the name of Jesus everyone
   in heaven, on earth, and under the earth might bow
      Jesus Christ is Lord, to the glory of God the Father.

Matthew 22:34–40
When the Pharisees heard that Jesus had left the Sadducees speechless, they met together. 35 One of them, a legal expert, tested him. 36 "Teacher, what is the greatest commandment in the Law?"
37 He replied, "You must love the Lord your God with all your heart, with all your being, and with all your mind. 38 This is the first and greatest commandment. 39 And the second is like it: You must love your neighbor as you love yourself. 40 All the Law and the Prophets depend on these two commands."

1

 thoughts on vocation

Which words jump out?

"But God first calls for us to survive.
This message of survival is one that deeply resonates in the Latinx community.
Whether it is surviving on the borderlands
or surviving the material conditions of our neighborhood,
God and our community challenge us and, even more importantly,
the next generation to survive.
This is the vocation of the disinherited, the oppressed, the marginalized
– all those who find themselves on the brink of death.
We are called to live."

– Dr. Patrick Reyes

muévete

Devotional:

"When it's time to say these hard things, I ask myself three things.
One: Did you mean it? Two: Can you defend it? Three: Did you say it with love?
If the answer is yes to all three, I say it and let the chips fall. That's important. That checkpoint with myself always tells me, 'Yes, you're supposed to do this.' Telling the truth—telling thoughtful truths—should not be a revolutionary act. Speaking truths to power should not be sacrificial, but they are. But I think if more of us chose to do this for the greater good, we'd be in better spaces than we are right now.

Speaking of the greater good, I think we commit ourselves to telling truths to build bridges to common ground, and bridges that aren't based on truth will collapse. So it is our job, it is our obligation, it is our duty to speak truth to power, to be the domino, not just when it's difficult—especially when it's difficult."
– Luvvie Ajayi

who's who

Luvvie Ajayi
Nigerian author, speaker, and digital strategist

What makes you uncomfortable? What fears do you have?

What helps you face and embrace being uncomfortable?

Spirit of the Living God, may this practice strengthen my spirit and equip me to dwell in your love.

week 1: open
thursday: spiritual discipline

 scripture

Matthew 6:9–13
Pray like this:
Our Father who is in heaven,
uphold the holiness of your name.
10 Bring in your kingdom
so that your will is done on earth as it's done in heaven.
11 Give us the bread we need for today.
12 Forgive us for the ways we have wronged you,
just as we also forgive those who have wronged us.
13 And don't lead us into temptation,
but rescue us from the evil one.

1 Corinthians 16:14
Everything should be done in love.

 liturgy of openness

Oh God, let my soul rise up to meet you, **as the day rises to meet the sun.**
Open me up to this day, **that I might encounter you.**
In my own being, **may I encounter you.**
In my neighbor and community, **may I see your face.**
In the challenges and disappointments, **may I know your presence.**
In the celebrations and excitement, **may I share your joy.**
May we be open. May we be broken open. **May we see you in a new way.**

◇◇◇◇◇◇◇◇◇ going deeper resource

Video: TED talk - Luvvie Ajayi "Get Comfortable with Being Uncomfortable"
Culture tends to celebrate comfort. Ajayi shares her experience and encouragement with leaning into discomfort.

41

week 1: open
friday experience

 friday experience

before the friday experience

What are you feeling as you head towards this experience?

Expectations? Hopes? Concerns?

Why did you choose this particular Friday Experience?

What questions will you ask?

after the friday experience

What justice issues and healing gifts did you notice?

What surprised you about this Experience?

Did you feel energized or depleted while learning about this work?

How might you incorporate what you're learning when you go back home?

Is this a vocation that interests you?

weekend check-in

No judgment, just noticing. How are you listening to your soul this week?

I was present and fully engaged in muévete ☐

I practiced centering prayer ☐

I did it afraid ☐

I intentionally thought about my friday experience ☐

What do I want to remember from this week? (write it in this space)

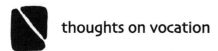 thoughts on vocation

It is also important to keep in mind that **vocation** is not only about **what we do** but about **who we are.**

—John Neafsey

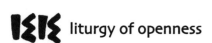 liturgy of openness

Oh God, let my soul rise up to meet you, **as the day rises to meet the sun.**
Open me up to this day, **that I might encounter you.**
In my own being, **may I encounter you.**
In my neighbor and community, **may I see your face.**
In the challenges and disappointments, **may I know your presence.**
In the celebrations and excitement, **may I share your joy.**
May we be open. May we be broken open. **May we see you in a new way.**

 muévete

What has remaining open looked like this week?

What types of vocations or callings are resonating with you?

What does your soul need to enter into rest?

What are you praying for this week?

Good Shepherd, lead me into rest. Lead me beside still waters. On this day, restore my soul.

1

1

1

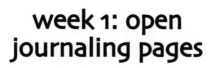

1

1

week 2: brokenness

Liturgy of a Broken Heart

The broken heart is a heavy heart, **how can we bear the weight of it alone?**
In our work and in our communities,
as we encounter wounds and injustice and tragedy,
God, give us a tribe and loving companions
to walk with in the journey of justice and healing.
Strengthen our spirits
So that when we fear and grieve,
We may remain present to ourselves and others,
Let the wisdom of the brokenness teach us,
And make us in the image of Love.
Give us tears to cry
And kind hands to dry
The eyes that wait to see the coming of your reign.
Lead us by our hearts
into openness and compassion,
Lead us through our tears
into purpose and gentleness,
Lead us through our grief
into justice and mercy.
Spirit of the resurrected Jesus, **be near to the brokenhearted.**

Prayers of the People

For the ones whose hearts break and whose eyes drip with salty tears...
...God, hear and hold our heavy hearts.

For the injustices and wounds we face that we cannot fix or find light in…
...God, hear and hold our heavy hearts.

For the ones we encounter in whose stories we long to find hope…
...God, hear and hold our heavy hearts.

For the ones who lead and benefit from systems of greed, corruption, and value profit over people…
...God, equip us to advocate for systems that benefit and empower all.

For the streams in the desert and the way made where there was no way…
...God, we pray for your imaginative healing that brings dry bones back to breathing life.

May we model the compassion of Jesus, the resilience of the Spirit, and the imaginative creativity of the Creator.
Amen.

week

2

brokenness

Lord's Prayer from the New Zealand Anglican Prayer book:

Eternal Spirit,
Earth-Maker, Pain-bearer, Life-giver
Source of all that is and all that shall be,
Father and Mother of us all,
Loving God who is in heaven:

The hallowing of your name echo through the universe!
The way of your justice be followed by people of the world!
Your heavenly will be done by all created beings!
Your commonwealth of peace and freedom sustain our hope and come on
earth.

With bread we need for today, feed us.
In the hurts we absorb from one another, forgive us.
In times of temptation and test, strengthen us.
From trials too great to endure, spare us.
From the grip of all that is evil, free us.

For you reign in the glory of the power that is love, now and forever.
May it be so. Amen.

week 2: brokenness
living in balance

 mind

 know thyself

 body

2

Knowing ourselves sounds easy. We're always with ourselves, right? Knowing ourselves is often the hardest journey we will take. It requires quieting the constant input around us, technology, responsibilities, others' expectations. We have voices in our head that can be negative, pressuring, or someone else's:

"Hurry up! Be perfect! Please this or that person! Do More! You're lazy, stupid, ugly, _____..."

Self-reflection requires stillness and raw honesty, which are counter to our culture. We are taught a rubric for our behavior and what we should be. This leads to self-reflection where we are constantly ranking ourselves against that rubric. Was that action good enough or a failure? Where am I in terms of gaining accomplishment and admiration? This kind of self-reflection doesn't allow room for curious reflection. In curious reflection, you can suspend all opinions of yourself, including your own. You can play and dive into the depths of who you really are and what you really want.
This **Relationship** with the Self fosters exponentially more creativity and often leads us to truly **Meaningful Work** that will bring immeasurably more satisfaction and health.

Exercise week two: morning pages
Write (do not type) three pages of stream of consciousness reflections immediately upon waking up in the morning.

Let it flow and don't stop writing until you're done with three pages. Write exactly what comes into your head. Don't edit. No need to punctuate or organize. UNCLUTTER your brain. If nothing comes up, write what you observe around you. Just don't stop writing.

Do this three days in a row this week upon waking. It won't be easy but it will show you a great deal about your inner thoughts and desires hidden beneath the noise and confines of your to do list. It will free your mind for greater focus and creativity.

who's who
this exercise comes from Julia Cameron filmmaker and author of *The Artist's Way*

Reflection:
Write about how easy or difficult this was for you.

Did you notice any patterns in what came up for you each morning?

Did you have any deeper understanding or clarity?

week 2: brokenness
living in balance

 spirit

the practice of noticing

Examen is the practice of noticing connections between events and feelings. Your response to the situation may be positive responses or negative. Often the negative feelings are great indicators for the need to go deeper.

Why did I react that way? What did that event provoke in me?

2

This is not about assigning blame to others, but rather looking for the piece of ourselves that felt threatened or elated in response to an event or conversation. Ask God to help you as you reflect on what happened.

Instructions:
Set aside ten minutes to think about the events of your day and notice which memory has the strongest feelings attached to it. Remember and relive that moment and how it felt, who was there and the interaction that occured. Name aloud the emotion you felt and your associations with that emotion. Ask God to help you know what you need in response to this experience.

Tips: this prayer can be used anytime you experience a strong emotional reaction to a situation.

Examen takes practice. You may need the assistance of a trusted counselor, pastor, or spiritual director to help you sort through the emotions or look for the movement of the Holy Spirit in these situations.

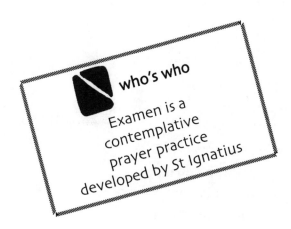

who's who

Examen is a contemplative prayer practice developed by St Ignatius

 going deeper resource

free app available:
Reimagining Examen
step by step, it walks you through the practice of examen using different themes each day

week 2: brokenness
monday: identity formation

 thoughts on vocation

> WE SHOULD CONSIDER THE QUESTION
> OF WHETHER THE INTRICACIES
> OF VOCATIONAL DISCERNMENT
> ARE JUST A LUXURY FOR THE PRIVILEGED CLASSES
> WHO ARE ECONOMICALLY SECURE ENOUGH
> TO BE ABLE TO WORRY ABOUT THINGS
> LIKE "AUTHENTICITY" OR "FOLLOWING THEIR BLISS."
> – JOHN NEAFSEY

liturgy of a broken heart

The broken heart is a heavy heart, **how can we bear the weight of it alone?**

In our work and in our communities,
as we encounter wounds and injustice and tragedy,
God, give us a tribe and loving companions
to walk with on the journey of justice and healing.

Strengthen our spirits
So that when we fear and grieve
We may remain present to ourselves and others,
Let the wisdom of brokenness teach us
And make us in the image of Love.

Give us tears to cry
And kind hands to dry
The eyes that wait to see the coming of your reign.

Lead us by our hearts
into openness and compassion,
Lead us through our tears
into purpose and gentleness,
Lead us through our grief
into justice and mercy.

Spirit of the resurrected Jesus, **be near the brokenhearted.**

 **scripture**

John 15:16
You didn't choose me, but I chose you and appointed you so that you could go and produce fruit and so that your fruit could last. As a result, whatever you ask the Father in my name, he will give you.

 **muévete**

Devotional:

> "If you tell me who you're envious of, what work you envy—
> I will tell you what you were meant to create.
> If you tell me what breaks your heart—
> I will tell you who you were meant to serve."
> – Glennon Doyle

> "If you want to find your passion, surrender to your heartbreak.
> Your heartbreak points toward a truer north..."
> – Umair Haque

who's who

Glennon Doyle
New York TImes
bestselling author,
activist and philanthropist

who's who

Umair Haque
author and
economic strategist

What things are weighing heavily on your heart?

With one week accomplished and a whole summer ahead of you, in what areas are you beginning to feel powerless, maybe even a sense of hopelessness?

Try not to run from it, try to sit and listen to it. Embrace the stirrings within you as the guides they are, trying to point you towards your purpose and calling. See where they lead.

Creator God, whose image I bear, help me to pay attention to what is occurring within me.

week 2: brokenness
tuesday: intentional community

thoughts on vocation

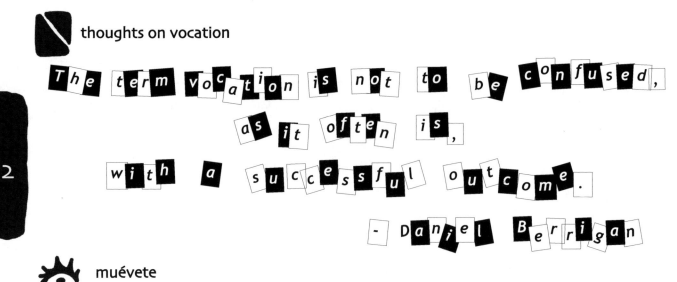

The term vocation is not to be confused, as it often is, with a successful outcome.

– Daniel Berrigan

muévete

Devotional:

"Everyone is gifted, and, as individuals share their gifts for the benefit of others,
they experience wholeness and the community becomes stronger."
– The Neighboring Movement, SoCe Life

A folk band, two couples (and one child) became an intentional community, committing to a rule of life focused on prayer, hospitality, and justice. Each week they gathered for a meal; each morning they gathered for prayer. They discussed how they were pursuing hospitality and justice as individuals and in their neighborhood. They began studying asset-based community development and got to know their neighbors' strengths and passions. The Neighboring Movement now teaches about the practices of neighboring and is doing revolutionary work to increase social capital, decrease loneliness, and nurture communal bonds in their area. All four adult members of the Neighboring Movement have attested that their work would not have been possible without the intentional community upon which it was founded. Each week this team had three peers to return to. When times were joyous or tough, whether they'd met an abundance of neighbors or had twenty doors slammed in their faces, they returned to the intentional community and were held in prayer, encouraged in hospitality, and nurtured towards a sense of justice. Without community, the things that break our hearts will likely leave us feeling overwhelmed by hopelessness and a sense of bitterness about our inability to impact the world for the better. Every vision needs the stamina to sustain it until it can come to fruition. Every endeavor needs a community of support that believes in the work.

How does your community help sustain you when you're feeling discouraged? Overwhelmed?

How can the weight of broken-heartedness be shared across your community?

Community of Love, Parent, Son, and Holy Spirit, teach me to see your image in my brother, sister, enemy, friend, and neighbor.

week 2: brokenness
tuesday: intentional community

 scripture

Ephesians 4:1–6
1 Therefore, as a prisoner for the Lord, I encourage you to live as people worthy of the call you received from God. 2 Conduct yourselves with all humility, gentleness, and patience. Accept each other with love, 3 and make an effort to preserve the unity of the Spirit with the peace that ties you together. 4 You are one body and one spirit, just as God also called you in one hope. 5 There is one Lord, one faith, one baptism, 6 and one God and Father of all, who is over all, through all, and in all.

1 Thessalonians 5:11–13
11 So continue encouraging each other and building each other up, just like you are doing already. 12 Brothers and sisters, we ask you to respect those who are working with you, leading you, and instructing you. 13 Think of them highly with love because of their work. Live in peace with each other.

ᛚᛣᛚᛣ liturgy of a broken heart

The broken heart is a heavy heart, **how can we bear the weight of it alone?**
In our work and in our communities,
as we encounter wounds and injustice and tragedy,
God, give us a tribe and loving companions
to walk with on the journey of justice and healing.
Strengthen our spirits
So that when we fear and grieve
We may remain present to ourselves and others,
Let the wisdom of brokenness teach us
And make us in the image of Love.
Give us tears to cry
And kind hands to dry
The eyes that wait to see the coming of your reign.
Lead us by our hearts
into openness and compassion,
Lead us through our tears
into purpose and gentleness,
Lead us through our grief
into justice and mercy.
Spirit of the resurrected Jesus, **be near the brokenhearted.**

who's who
The Neighboring Movement in South Central Wichita, Kansas, is doing revolutionary work to increase social capital, decrease lonliness and nurture communal bonds

week 2: brokenness
wednesday: servant leadership

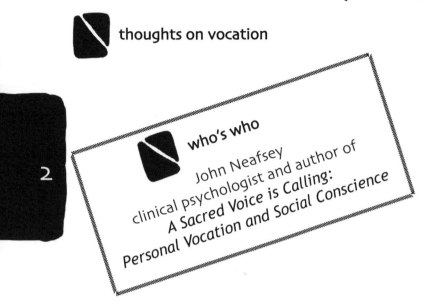

thoughts on vocation

who's who
John Neafsey
clinical psychologist and author of
*A Sacred Voice is Calling:
Personal Vocation and Social Conscience*

The vocational question,
it seems, has to do with **identifying**
those for whom we hurt.
To which of God's people
do our hearts seem to go out to most?
Whose sufferings and aspirations
are speaking or calling to us?
Where, or to whom,
does our heart seem to be leading us?

– John Neafsey

liturgy of a broken heart

The broken heart is a heavy heart, **how can we bear the weight of it alone?**

In our work and in our communities,
as we encounter wounds and injustice and tragedy,
**God, give us a tribe and loving companions
to walk with on the journey of justice and healing.**

Strengthen our spirits
So that when we fear and grieve
We may remain present to ourselves and others,
**Let the wisdom of brokenness teach us
And make us in the image of Love.**

Give us tears to cry
And kind hands to dry
The eyes that wait to see the coming of your reign.

who's who
Susan Cain
author of
*Quiet: The Power of Introverts in a
World that Can't Stop Talking*

Lead us by our hearts
into openness and compassion,
Lead us through our tears
into purpose and gentleness,
Lead us through our grief
into justice and mercy.
Spirit of the resurrected Jesus, **be near the brokenhearted.**

week 2: brokenness
wednesday: servant leadership

 **scripture**

Jeremiah 31:21, 25
21 Set up markers,
　put up signs;
　think about the road you have traveled,
　　the path you have taken.
Return, virgin Israel;
　return to these towns of yours.
25 I will strengthen the weary and renew those who are weak.

 **muévete**

Devotional:

> "You don't have to stand up for your rights to get justice,
> sometimes you can sit for your rights like Rosa Parks."
> - Harmon Okinyo, Goodreads librarian

> "I had always imagined Rosa Parks as a stately woman with a bold temperament, someone who could easily stand up to a busload of glowering passengers. But when she died in 2005 at the age of ninety-two, the flood of obituaries recalled her as soft-spoken, sweet, and small in stature. They said she was 'timid and shy' but had 'the courage of a lion.' They were full of phrases like 'radical humility' and 'quiet fortitude.'"
> - Susan Cain

What assumptions do you have about servant leadership?

Who is qualified to serve? What gifts are best?

In the case of Rosa Parks, her leadership began, not by standing up, but by sitting still. She said of her actions that day on the bus, "People always say that I didn't give up my seat because I was tired, but that isn't true. No, the only tired I was, was tired of giving in."

Service and leadership can be about gifts. It can also be about where you're standing (or sitting).

What is one thing I am broken hearted about?

What is one step I can take to address that?

Jesus, Servant of the Lord, empower us in the gifts we bring. Equip us to lead from where we are.

week 2: brokenness
thursday: spiritual discipline

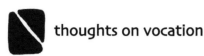 thoughts on vocation

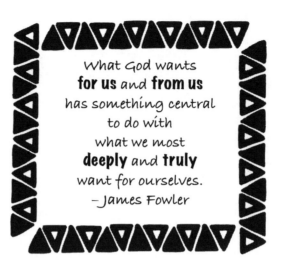

What God wants
for us and **from us**
has something central
to do with
what we most
deeply and **truly**
want for ourselves.
—James Fowler

 muévete

Devotional:
"There are three things we all must learn to do if what Keats called our 'world of pains and troubles' is to become a school of the Spirit, the heart, the soul. First, acknowledge and name our suffering honestly and openly to ourselves and to others. Second, we must move directly to the heart of it, allowing ourselves to feel the pain fully...The only way to transform suffering into something life-giving is to enter into it so deeply that we learn what it has to teach us and come out on the other side. Third, we must create a micro-climate of quietude around ourselves, allowing the turmoil to settle and an inner quietude to emerge, so 'that of God within us' can help us find our way through."
– Parker Palmer, from "The Broken-Open Heart"

Consider curiosity as a spiritual discipline.

Engaging with others from a space of curiosity can lead to deeper relationships, calmer conversations, new insights, and a broader perspective. Approaching ourselves with curiosity about our reactions and feelings in response to things can lead to deeper understanding and wiser decisions.

In what ways can you practice the spiritual discipline of curiosity this week?

Spirit of the Living God, may this practice strengthen my spirit and equip me to dwell in your love.

week 2: brokenness
thursday: spiritual discipline

 scripture

Isaiah 43:2

2 When you pass through the waters, I will be with you;
   when through the rivers, they won't sweep
over you. When you walk through the fire, you won't be scorched
   and flame won't burn you.

Isaiah 43:5

5 Don't fear,
   I am with you.
From the east I'll bring your children;
   from the west I'll gather you.

Isaiah 43:16–19

16 The Lord says—who makes a way in the sea
   and a path in the mighty waters,
17   who brings out chariot and horse,
   army and battalion;
   they will lie down together and will not rise;
   they will be extinguished, extinguished like a wick.
18 Don't remember the prior things;
   don't ponder ancient history.
19 Look! I'm doing a new thing;
   now it sprouts up; don't you recognize it?
I'm making a way in the desert,
   paths in the wilderness.

who's who
Parker Palmer
author, educator and activist
Founder and Senior Director of the
Center for Courage & Renewal

 going deeper resource

Reading: Parker Palmer, "The Broken Open Heart"
Article from Weavings journal about living and working in the tragic gap
https://www.couragerenewal.org/PDFs/PJP-WeavingsArticle-Broken-OpenHeart.pdf

Video: TED talk - Brene Brown "The power of vulnerability"
Brown is a shame researcher who writes about connection, belonging, courage, and empathy. This is a moving talk about the difficult and worthwhile journey towards vulnerability

week 2: brokenness
friday experience

 friday experience

before the friday experience

What are you feeling as you head towards this experience?

Expectations? Hopes? Concerns?

Why did you choose this particular Friday Experience?

What questions will you ask?

after the friday experience

What justice issues and healing gifts did you notice?

What surprised you about this Experience?

Did you feel energized or depleted while learning about this work?

How might you incorporate what you're learning when you go back home?

Is this a vocation that interests you?

weekend check-in

No judgment, just noticing. How are you listening to your soul this week?

I was present and fully engaged in muévete ☐

I practiced examen ☐

I wrote morning pages this week ☐

I intentionally thought about my friday experience ☐

What do I want to remember from this week? (write it in this space)

week 2: brokenness
fifth day: Sabbath rest

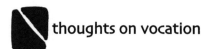 thoughts on vocation

The promise and vulnerability of emerging adulthood
lie in the experience of the birth of critical awareness and consequently
in the dissolution and recomposition of the meaning of self, other, world, and "God."
In the process of human becoming, this task of achieving critical thought
and discerning its consequences for one's sense of meaning and purpose has enormous implications
for the years of adulthood to follow.
Emerging adulthood is rightfully a time of asking big questions and crafting worthy dreams.
~ Sharon Daloz Parks

liturgy of brokenness

The broken heart is a heavy heart, **how can we bear the weight of it alone?**

In our work and in our communities,
as we encounter wounds and injustice
and tragedy,
**God, give us a tribe and loving companions
to walk with on the journey of justice and healing.**

Give us tears to cry
And kind hands to dry
**The eyes that wait to see the coming of your
reign.**

Strengthen our spirits
So that when we fear and grieve
We may remain present
to ourselves and others,
**Let the wisdom of brokenness teach us,
And make us in the image of Love.**

Lead us by our hearts
into openness and compassion,
Lead us through our tears
into purpose and gentleness,
Lead us through our grief
into justice and mercy.

Spirit of the resurrected Jesus, **be near the brokenhearted.**

muévete
Devotional:
What has broken your heart this week?

What types of vocations or callings are resonating with you?

What does your soul need to enter into rest?

What are you praying for this week?

Good Shepherd, lead me into rest. Lead me beside still waters. On this day, restore my soul.

2

2

2

2

2

week 3: show up

Liturgy of Showing Up

God, as your Spirit first hovered over the waters in chaos,
As Jesus entered into the flesh and bones of the world,
As the Spirit comes to be our Advocate,
Teach us how to show up to ourselves, to each other,
and to your presence in the world.
Lead us into our gifts and stories,
show us how we can contribute and arrive.
Lead us towards the tears and stories of others,
show us how we can best listen and understand.
Lead us towards awareness of the systems of power and economics,
show us how we can spend and live with intentionality and justice.
Lead us towards the goodness in all people,
show us how to honor all of your creatures and creation.

Prayers of the People

For the invitations we encounter within us,
For the gifts you've given us,
For the ways our unique perspective and wisdom is called up...
...God, guide us to know what you have created is good.

For the invitations in our community, in our neighbors and peers and the children we encounter,
For the beauty of the body and the diversity of the abilities,
...God, help us to lean in with gratitude and curiosity.

For the ways we are shifting and changing,
For the prayers spoken and unspoken,
For the surprises along the way this summer...
...God, help us to arrive here, to this place, among you and among each other.

For the stories we hear,
For the histories everyone brings,
For the tension as iron sharpens iron...
...God, lead us into love towards all that you have created.

For the struggles that need our support,
For the strengths that need to be witnessed,
For the connections that need to be made,
For the hope that needs to be told...
...God, help us to pay attention.

Amen.

week

3

show up

week 3: show up
living in balance

 mind

top ten

 body

> Setting goals
> is the first step
> in turning the invisible
> into the visible.
> - Tony Robbins

We cannot reach a goal we do not have. One purpose of reflection is to understand ourselves more fully: listen to our truest desires and the voice of the Holy Spirit, so we can take creative action. This enables us to participate with God and realize our dreams and fosters **Meaningful Work** through **Relationship** with God and our Self.

3

Exercise week three: Top Ten
Based on your self-reflection last week, make a list of your Top Ten goals you want to TAKE AC-TION on to create change in your life. This kind of **Physical Activity** will catapult you from analy-sis paralysis to realizing optimal holistic health.

Make a list of your top ten goals in order of importance.

Make sure your goals are SMART: Specific, Measurable, Achievable, Relevant, Time-Specific.

As you accomplish a goal, cross it off, add another goal and re-prioritize your list in order of impor-tance. You will always have ten goals you are working to achieve, which makes it much harder to get stuck. Tape a copy of your Top Ten to your mirror or some place you look every day.

1.

2.

3.

4.

5.

6.

7.

8.

9.

10.

Reflection:
Did you accomplish any of your Top Ten goals this week?

Were you more likely to act having them written, prioritized, and within sight?

week 3: show up
living in balance

 spirit

the practice of praying for others

Intercessory prayer asks us to pray for other people: those we love and those we struggle to love.

In Hebrew, the word for "enemy" comes from the same root as "to cloak." When Jesus teaches us to pray for our enemies, he is asking us to pray that the presence of God in that person be uncloaked. Another way to say it: May the Spirit of God become visible in that person.

What is my hope for this person?
What gift would bring this person greater openness to the life-giving Spirit of God?

Intercessory prayer can be a powerful tool in altering our perception of others. We all have various social groups we influence and are influenced by. Holding these ever-widening circles in prayer for healing, growth and transformation both affects the possibilities within those spheres, and also connects us to them more strongly as we offer positive intentional thought and hopes for them.

3

Instructions:
Draw a number of connected circles, beginning with yourself, then your closest family or friend group, and so on through your community, to the larger Universe. As you draw them, fill in the names of people that come to mind and offer a prayer for that person or group. It may be as simple as naming them, or as complex as asking for something vaguely specific like healing, wisdom, peace, or blessing. Remember to include the difficult people, but refrain from assuming you know what they need and keep it open.

Who is in my community?

(Me)

Who is my neighbor?

What are my longings for my neighbors?

week 3: show up
monday: identity formation

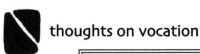 thoughts on vocation

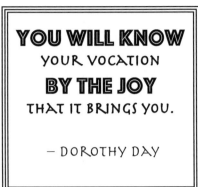

YOU WILL KNOW YOUR VOCATION **BY THE JOY** THAT IT BRINGS YOU.

— DOROTHY DAY

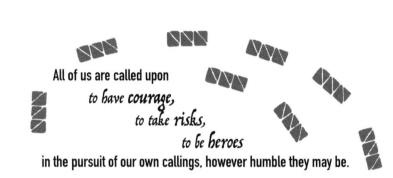

All of us are called upon *to have courage, to take risks, to be heroes* in the pursuit of our own callings, however humble they may be.

— John Neafsey

3 muévete

Devotional:

"Discovering vocation does not mean scrambling toward some prize just beyond my reach but accepting the treasure of true self I already possess. Vocation does not come from a voice out there calling me to be something I am not. It comes from a voice in here calling me to be the person I was born to be, to fulfill the original selfhood given me at birth by God."
– Thomas Merton

who's who

Thomas Merton American Trappist monk, writer, theologian and mystic

Calling does not have to be a lifetime assignment; it can be right where you're standing, and it can be for the next six minutes. Calling can begin right where we are, with what we have, as who we are. What is your inner voice saying? It may not be a voice or specific words, perhaps it is simply a knowing, an awareness about yourself. In twelve step programs, they speak of "the next right thing."

Without asking anyone else what you should do, what is the next right thing for you to do today?

When you think of who you were born to be, what ideas come to mind? Consider what is good about where you already are.

Creator God, whose image I bear, help me to pay attention to what is occurring within me.

week 3: show up
monday: identity formation

 scripture

Genesis 1:1–2
1 When God began to create the heavens and the earth— 2 the earth was without shape or form, it was dark over the deep sea, and God's wind swept over the waters

ヒ彡|ヒ liturgy of showing up

God, as your Spirit first hovered over the waters in chaos,
As Jesus entered into the flesh and bones of the world,
As the Spirit comes to be our Advocate,
Teach us how to show up to ourselves, to each other,
and to your presence in the world.
Lead us into our gifts and stories,
show us how we can contribute and arrive.
Lead us towards the tears and stories of others,
show us how we can best listen and understand.
Lead us towards awareness of the systems of power and economics,
show us how we can spend and live with intentionality and justice.
Lead us towards the goodness in all people,
show us how to honor all of your creatures and creation.

◈◈◈◈◈◈◈◈ going deeper resource

Reading: Elizabeth Cady Stanton, "Solitude of Self"
Stanton addresses the Committee of the Judiciary of the United States Congress on women's rights and equality on January 18, 1892
http://etc.usf.edu/lit2go/185/civil-rights-and-conflict-in-the-united-states-selected-speeches/4854/solitude-of-self-address-before-the-committee-of-the-judiciary-of-the-united-states-congress-january-18-1892/

Video: Cleo Wade. "Want to change the world? Start by being brave enough to care"
Artist and poet Cleo Wade offers insight on a courageous and meaningful life.
TED talk at TEDWomen2017
https://www.ted.com/talks/cleo_wade_want_to_change_the_world_start_by_being_brave_enough_to_care

week 3: show up
tuesday: intentional community

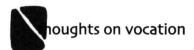houghts on vocation

> *Faith is intimately linked with a sense of* **vocation** – *awareness of living one's life* **aligned** *with a larger frame of* **purpose** *and* **significance.**
>
> - Sharon Daloz Parks

 muévete

Devotional:

> "There are many things that can only be seen through eyes that have cried."
> – Archbishop Oscar Romero, Fourth Archbishop of San Salvador,
> spoke out against poverty, social injustice, assassinations, and torture

> "As members of the body of Christ, we are called to be accomplices, not allies,
> in the work of [racial] justice."
> – Marilyn Nash

In community, we are confronted with the realities, experiences, and perspectives of others. We may not walk their same road, but we have joined our paths with theirs, and so we learn their story. What is your community (everyone you encounter) teaching you this week that you wouldn't see without them?

who's who

Marilyn Nash
campus minister
for social justice
at Seattle University

In what ways can you show up for their story, even if it doesn't directly affect you?

What are you seeing through another's eyes?

Community of Love, Parent, Son, and Holy Spirit, teach me to see your image in my brother, sister, enemy, friend, and neighbor.

week 3: show up
tuesday: intentional community

 scripture

Luke 4:18–19
18 The Spirit of the Lord is upon me,
   because the Lord has anointed me.
He has sent me to preach good news to the poor,
   to proclaim release to the prisoners
   and recovery of sight to the blind,
   to liberate the oppressed,
19 and to proclaim the year of the Lord's favor.

*What road
am I on?*

3

liturgy of showing up

God, as your Spirit first hovered over the waters in chaos,
As Jesus entered into the flesh and bones of the world,
As the Spirit comes to be our Advocate,
**Teach us how to show up to ourselves, to each other,
and to your presence in the world.**
Lead us into our gifts and stories,
show us how we can contribute and arrive.
Lead us towards the tears and stories of others,
show us how we can best listen and understand.
Lead us towards awareness of the systems of power and economics,
show us how we can spend and live with intentionality and justice.
Lead us towards the goodness in all people,
show us how to honor all of your creatures and creation.

week 3: show up
wednesday: servant leadership

 thoughts on vocation

"Vocation implies a teleology (from the Greek telos, 'purpose' or 'goal'), insofar as our callings are meant to achieve some goal or purpose. That purpose may be quite focused and immediate, such as attending to a person in need or being available to a friend; or it may shape the overall trajectory of our lives, such as being faithful in love and committed to justice. But in all cases, our callings ask us to become something more than we already are; this implies movement, change, and transformation in light of the goods we are trying to achieve."
– Paul J. Wadell

muévete

If you have come here to help me, you are wasting your time. But if you have come because your liberation is bound up with mine, then let us work together.

– Lilla Watson

who's who

Lilla Watson
indigenous Australian
visual artist, activist, and academic working in the field of women's issues and epistemology

Devotional:
Helping can often perpetuate an imbalance of power. One party becomes the savior, another becomes the one in need of rescuing. Education is a great way to combat and undermine this power hierarchy: educate someone, and you equip and empower them to eventually become their own teacher, and to give back to others.

In what ways are you noticing systems of power at work here? What are some helpful and unhelpful responses to that power you're noticing?

Jesus, Servant of the Lord, empower us in the gifts we bring. Equip us to lead from where we are.

week 3: show up
wednesday: servant leadership

 scripture

John 13:1–17

Before the Festival of Passover, Jesus knew that his time had come to leave this world and go to the Father. Having loved his own who were in the world, he loved them fully.
2 Jesus and his disciples were sharing the evening meal. The devil had already provoked Judas, Simon Iscariot's son, to betray Jesus. 3 Jesus knew the Father had given everything into his hands and that he had come from God and was returning to God. 4 So he got up from the table and took off his robes. Picking up a linen towel, he tied it around his waist. 5 Then he poured water into a washbasin and began to wash the disciples' feet, drying them with the towel he was wearing. 6 When Jesus came to Simon Peter, Peter said to him, "Lord, are you going to wash my feet?"
7 Jesus replied, "You don't understand what I'm doing now, but you will understand later."
8 "No!" Peter said. "You will never wash my feet!"
Jesus replied, "Unless I wash you, you won't have a place with me."
9 Simon Peter said, "Lord, not only my feet but also my hands and my head!"
10 Jesus responded, "Those who have bathed need only to have their feet washed, because they are completely clean. You disciples are clean, but not every one of you." 11 He knew who would betray him. That's why he said, "Not every one of you is clean."
12 After he washed the disciples' feet, he put on his robes and returned to his place at the table. He said to them, "Do you know what I've done for you? 13 You call me 'Teacher' and 'Lord,' and you speak correctly, because I am. 14 If I, your Lord and teacher, have washed your feet, you too must wash each other's feet.

15 I have given you an example: Just as I have done, you also must do. 16 I assure you, servants aren't greater than their master, nor are those who are sent greater than the one who sent them. 17 Since you know these things, you will be happy if you do them.

【【【 liturgy of showing up

God, as your Spirit first hovered over the waters in chaos,
As Jesus entered into the flesh and bones of the world,
As the Spirit comes to be our Advocate,
Teach us how to show up to ourselves, to each other,
and to your presence in the world.
Lead us into our gifts and stories,
show us how we can contribute and arrive.
Lead us towards the tears and stories of others,
show us how we can best listen and understand.
Lead us towards awareness of the systems of power and economics,
show us how we can spend and live with intentionality and justice.
Lead us towards the goodness in all people,
show us how to honor all of your creatures and creation.

week 3: show up
thursday: spiritual discipline

 thoughts on vocation

Discernment
pertains to more than just
our efforts to evaluate and interpret
the complex crosscurrents
of our inner experience.
It also involves
cultivating a critical consciousness
about our social reality
so that we can
discover our social responsibilities within it
and
decide how best to use our energies and talents
for the common good.

- John Neafsey

 muévete

Devotional:

"The transcendence that the church preaches is not alienation; it is not going to heaven to think about eternal life and forget about the problems on earth. It's a transcendence from the human heart. It is entering into the reality of a child, of the poor, of those wearing rags, of the sick, of a hovel, of a shack. It is going to share with them. And from the very heart of misery, of this situation, to transcend it, to elevate it, to promote it, and to say to them, 'You aren't trash. You aren't marginalized.' It is to say exactly the opposite, 'You are valuable.'"
- Archbishop Oscar Romero

It can be hard when we confront pain and systems of injustice to stay present, to enter in, to not look away. It can be tempting to run for the hills in retreat. If we do not know how to fix it, it can be difficult to stay and look. But it is very important that we do, for in staying and engaging, by showing up and entering in, we recognize the dignity in every human being, we recognize the worth in everyone's story.

 **who's who**

Oscar Romero
Fourth Archbishop of San Salvador
spoke out against poverty, social injustice,
assassinations, and torture

What invitations do you see to "enter in" as a spiritual discipline?

Spirit of the Living God, may this practice strengthen my spirit and equip me to dwell in your love.

week 3: show up
thursday: spiritual discipline

 scripture

Romans 8:26

In the same way, the Spirit comes to help our weakness. We don't know what we should pray, but the Spirit himself pleads our case with unexpressed groans.

spiritual discipline: entering in

liturgy of showing up

God, as your Spirit first hovered over the waters in chaos,
As Jesus entered into the flesh and bones of the world,
As the Spirit comes to be our Advocate,
Teach us how to show up to ourselves, to each other,
and to your presence in the world.
Lead us into our gifts and stories,
show us how we can contribute and arrive.
Lead us towards the tears and stories of others,
show us how we can best listen and understand.
Lead us towards awareness of the systems of power and economics,
show us how we can spend and live with intentionality and justice.
Lead us towards the goodness in all people,
show us how to honor all of your creatures and creation.

week 3: show up
friday experience

 **friday experience**

before the friday experience

What are you feeling as you head towards this experience?

Expectations? Hopes? Concerns?

Why did you choose this particular Friday Experience?

What questions will you ask?

after the friday experience

What justice issues and healing gifts did you notice?

What surprised you about this Experience?

Did you feel energized or depleted while learning about this work?

How might you incorporate what you're learning when you go back home?

Is this a vocation that interests you?

 **weekend check-in**

No judgment, just noticing. How are you listening to your soul this week?

I was present and fully engaged in muévete ☐

I practiced intercessory concentric circle prayer ☐

I listed my ten action goals ☐

I intentionally thought about my friday experience ☐

What do I want to remember from this week? (write it in this space)

week 3: show up
fifth day: Sabbath rest

IF YOU ARE
what you should be
THEN YOU WILL
set the world on fire.

~ St. Catherine of Siena

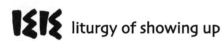 liturgy of showing up

God, as your Spirit first hovered over the waters in chaos,
As Jesus entered into the flesh and bones of the world,
As the Spirit comes to be our Advocate,
**Teach us how to show up to ourselves, to each other,
and to your presence in the world.**
Lead us into our gifts and stories,
show us how we can contribute and arrive.
Lead us towards the tears and stories of others,
show us how we can best listen and understand.
Lead us towards awareness of the systems of power and economics,
show us how we can spend and live with intentionality and justice.
Lead us towards the goodness in all people,
show us how to honor all of your creatures and creation.

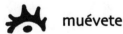 muévete

Devotional:
What has showing up looked like this week?

What types of vocations or callings are resonating with you?

What does your soul need to enter into rest?

What are you praying for this week?

Good Shepherd, lead me into rest. Lead me beside still waters. On this day, restore my soul.

3

3

3

3

Liturgy of Listening

Listen, says the Lord God.
Pay attention to my voice.
The sheep know the voice of the shepherd,
This does not necessarily mean the words are clear.
God desires mercy and not sacrifices,
Temples that shelter and protect the marginalized,
Eventually, the lion shall lie down with the lamb.
Jesus comes, not a prince but a pauper,
Stands and sits with sinners,
Shocks the leaders
Shatters expectations.
Stirs up healing and trouble on the Sabbath.
Resurrection and life ever-defeating death
Behold, God is on the move.

Prayers of the People

A moment of silence, to hear the voices of the ones we've encountered this week.
What stories have they told us? (silence.)
God, we give you thanks.

A moment of silence, for the ones who are not being heard. For the ones who cry out and eagerly await a new story and space of hope. (Silence.)
God in your mercy, hear our cries.

A moment of silence, for our internal voice to speak. For our thoughts and feelings to arise. For our fears and loves to teach us about ourselves. (Silence.)
God, our Creator, introduce us to ourselves.

A moment of silence, to hear our neighbors and our community. What condition is the Body of Christ in? (Silence.)
Jesus, help us abandon rigid doctrines for the sake of following you into healing and justice.

A moment of silence, for our churches, our leaders, our systems. (Silence.)
Spirit, lead us towards these people and into these places, such that we may be part of the work *of* compassion and justice.

A moment of silence, for all that God hopes to do in this community, in this summer, and in our lives and for the sake of the blessing of all people. (Silence.)
Good shepherd, lead us onward.

Amen.

week

4

listen

The Prayer of Saint Francis

Lord make me an instrument of your peace
Where there is hatred let me sow love
Where there is injury, pardon
Where there is doubt, faith
Where there is despair, hope
Where there is darkness, light
And where there is sadness, joy

O divine master grant that I may
not so much seek to be consoled as to console
to be understood as to understand
To be loved as to love
For it is in giving that we receive
it is in pardoning that we are pardoned
And it's in dying that we are born to eternal life
Amen

week 4:listen
living in balance

 mind

 listening

 body

Our power of imagination determines what we are capable of in mind, body, and spirit. In the words of Albert Einstein, "Imagination is more important than knowledge. For knowledge is limited, whereas imagination embraces the entire world, stimulating progress, giving birth to evolution."

True listening and observation of our environment and ourself keeps our imagination alive and open to wonder. Where have you limited yourself by confining your mind to easy knowledge at the expense of imagination? This is the edge where you stopped listening. This is your starting point of expansion in Spiritual Practice.

FAITH THAT MOVES MOUNTAINS is a faith that expands horizons; **IT DOES NOT BRING US INTO A SMALLER WORLD** of easy answers, **BUT A LARGER ONE** where there is **ROOM FOR WONDER.**

- Rich Mullins

4

Exercise week four: listening

Outward Listening: Observational Walking Meditation
Take a silent walk outdoors for fifteen minutes. Do this alone. Walk as slowly as you possibly can.   Set a timer.
Observe the world around you as you walk. What surprises you, draws your curiosity?
Use all your senses. Close your eyes and feel the elements of temperature, wind, light around you.
        Listen. Smell.
Notice the movement of your mind. When a thought comes, consciously let it go and train your senses to the experience of the world around you.

Reflection:
Write about your experience of bearing witness to your environment. What drew you in and surprised you? Did anything you observed inspire your imagination or shift a perspective?

Inward Listening: Mirror Meditation
Sit or stand in front of a mirror for ten minutes. Set a timer.
Look at yourself the entire time. Not in vanity, but curiosity.
Listen to the thoughts and feelings that rise in you. Notice the pattern of your mind and emotions.
How does this feel in your body? Notice your physical response as you reflect on yourself.

Reflection:
Write about your experience of bearing witness to yourself. What did you notice about the movement of your thoughts and emotions? How did those thoughts and emotions manifest in your physical body? Did anything you observed inspire your imagination or shift a perspective?

week 4: listen
living in balance

the practice of creativity and imagination

A labyrinth is not a maze; there is only one path and no getting lost. The labyrinth path is a metaphor for our life journey with its twists and turns as we take one step at a time towards the inevitable center. The center can represent God, a decision, or a destination of some kind.

Instructions:

Beginning at the outer entrance, use your finger to follow the path through the labyrinth. As you go, think about what you are seeking today. At the center, spend a few moments in silence. Notice how you feel. Symbolically lay down burdens at the center by drawing a symbol or a mark there. To finish, you may either follow the path back out or simply lift your finger off the page.

4

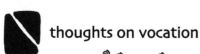 thoughts on vocation

THE WORLD IS FULL OF PEOPLE
who seem to have listened to the wrong voice
and are NOW ENGAGED IN LIFE-WORK
in which they find no pleasure or purpose
and WHO RUN THE RISK OF SUDDENLY REALIZING
some day that THEY HAVE SPENT THE ONLY YEARS
they are ever going to get in this world
DOING SOMETHING *which could not matter less*
to themselves or to anyone else...
work THAT SEEMS SIMPLY IRRELEVANT
not only to the great human needs and issues of our time but also
TO THEIR OWN NEED TO GROW AND DEVELOP AS HUMANS.

– Frederick Buechner

4

liturgy of listening

Listen, says the Lord God.
Pay attention to my voice.
The sheep know the voice of the shepherd,
This does not necessarily mean the words are clear.
God desires mercy and not sacrifices,
Temples that shelter and protect the marginalized,
Eventually, the lion shall lie down with the lamb.
Jesus comes not a prince but a pauper,
Stands and sits with sinners,
Shocks the leaders
Shatters expectations.
Stirs up healing and trouble on the Sabbath.
Resurrection and life, ever-defeating death,
Behold, God is on the move.

week 4: listen
monday: identity formation

 scripture

John 11:33–35
33 When Jesus saw her crying and the Jews who had come with her crying also, he was deeply disturbed and troubled. 34 He asked, "Where have you laid him?"
They replied, "Lord, come and see."
35 Jesus began to cry.

Micah 6:8
He has told you, human one, what is good and what the Lord requires from you: to do justice, embrace faithful love, and walk humbly with your God.

 muévete

Devotional:
"May God bless us with discomfort at easy answers, half-truths, and superficial relationships,
so that we may live deep within our hearts.
May God bless us with anger at injustice, oppression, and exploitation of people,
so that we may work for justice, freedom, and peace.
May God bless us with tears to shed for those who suffer from pain, rejection, hunger, and war,
so that we may reach out our hands to comfort them
and turn their pain into joy.
And may God bless us with enough foolishness to believe
that we can make a difference in this world,
so that we can do what others claim cannot be done,
to bring justice and kindness to all our children and the poor."
– A Franciscan Blessing

In what ways are you noticing discomfort, anger, tears, and perhaps even foolishness?

What is stirring within you in this work?

What feels like blessing? What doesn't?

Jesus stood beside the poor and the powerless; Micah tells us that God is pleased with humility and work for justice. This is hard work, and yet we follow and stand beside a God who, in the form of flesh and spirit, stands beside those who mourn, struggle, and hope for liberation. Know that where you stand is a place of blessing as the work for justice and healing continues.

Creator God, whose image I bear, help me to pay attention to what is occurring within me.

week 4:listen
tuesday: intentional community

 thoughts on vocation

Shug: Here's the thing…The thing I believe. God is inside you and inside everybody else. You come into the world with God. But only them that search inside for it find it. And sometimes it just manifest itself even if you not looking, or don't know what you looking for. Trouble do it for most folks, I think.

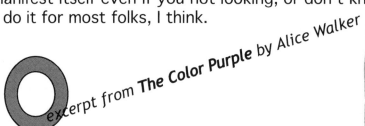

*excerpt from **The Color Purple** by Alice Walker*

liturgy of listening

4

Listen, says the Lord God.
Pay attention to my voice.
The sheep know the voice of the shepherd,
This does not necessarily mean the words are clear.
God desires mercy and not sacrifices,
Temples that shelter and protect the marginalized,
Eventually, the lion shall lie down with the lamb.
Jesus comes not a prince but a pauper,
Stands and sits with sinners,
Shocks the leaders
Shatters expectations.
Stirs up healing and trouble on the Sabbath.
Resurrection and life, ever-defeating death,
Behold, God is on the move.

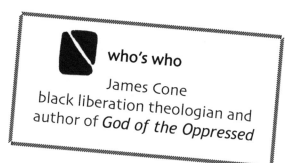 **who's who**

James Cone
black liberation theologian and author of *God of the Oppressed*

TRY IT OUT What names and images of God are most comfortable for me?
Take an opportunity to poll a peer, friend, or even one of the neighborhood kids. What names and images for God are most comfortable for them?

week 4: listen
tuesday: intentional community

 scripture

Luke 10:25–37

25 A legal expert stood up to test Jesus. "Teacher," he said, "what must I do to gain eternal life?"
26 Jesus replied, "What is written in the Law? How do you interpret it?"
27 He responded, "You must love the Lord your God with all your heart, with all your being, with all your strength, and with all your mind, and love your neighbor as yourself."
28 Jesus said to him, "You have answered correctly. Do this and you will live."
29 But the legal expert wanted to prove that he was right, so he said to Jesus, "And who is my neighbor?"
30 Jesus replied, "A man went down from Jerusalem to Jericho. He encountered thieves, who stripped him naked, beat him up, and left him near death. 31 Now it just so happened that a priest was also going down the same road. When he saw the injured man, he crossed over to the other side of the road and went on his way. 32 Likewise, a Levite came by that spot, saw the injured man, and crossed over to the other side of the road and went on his way. 33 A Samaritan, who was on a journey, came to where the man was. But when he saw him, he was moved with compassion. 34 The Samaritan went to him and bandaged his wounds, tending them with oil and wine. Then he placed the wounded man on his own donkey, took him to an inn, and took care of him. 35 The next day, he took two full days' worth of wages and gave them to the innkeeper. He said, 'Take care of him, and when I return, I will pay you back for any additional costs.' 36 What do you think? Which one of these three was a neighbor to the man who encountered thieves?"
37 Then the legal expert said, "The one who demonstrated mercy toward him."
Jesus told him, "Go and do likewise."

John 13:34-35

34 "I give you a new commandment: Love each other. Just as I have loved you, so you also must love each other. 35 This is how everyone will know that you are my disciples, when you love each other."

 muévete

Devotional:

"Through the reading of scripture, the people hear other stories about Jesus
that enable them to move beyond the privateness of their own stories."
– James H. Cone, in **God of the Oppressed**

"Indeed our survival and liberation depend upon our recognition of the truth when it is spoken and lived by the people. If we cannot recognize the truth, then it cannot liberate us from untruth. To know the truth is to appropriate it, for it is not mainly reflection and theory. Truth is divine action entering our lives and creating the human action of liberation."
– James H. Cone, in **God of the Oppressed**

In what ways do others in the community reveal aspects of God to you?

Where is God showing up in places that you may not have expected?

Community of Love, Parent, Son, and Holy Spirit, teach me to see your image in my brother, sister, enemy, friend, and neighbor.

wednesday: servant leadership

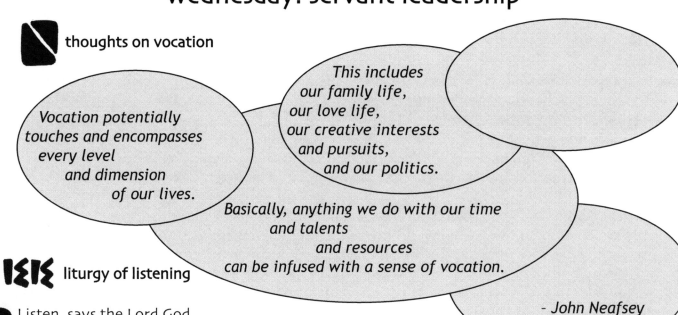

 thoughts on vocation

Vocation potentially touches and encompasses every level and dimension of our lives.

This includes our family life, our love life, our creative interests and pursuits, and our politics.

Basically, anything we do with our time and talents and resources can be infused with a sense of vocation.

- John Neafsey

ƖƐƖƐ liturgy of listening

4

Listen, says the Lord God.
Pay attention to my voice.
The sheep know the voice of the shepherd,
This does not necessarily mean the words are clear.
God desires mercy and not sacrifices,
Temples that shelter and protect the marginalized,
Eventually, the lion shall lie down with the lamb.
Jesus comes not a prince but a pauper,
Stands and sits with sinners,
Shocks the leaders
Shatters expectations.
Stirs up healing and trouble on the Sabbath.
Resurrection and life, ever-defeating death,
Behold, God is on the move.

muévete

Devotional:

> "There is good news, and it comes in the vulnerable,
> unexpected package of a baby
> born into poverty in an occupied land."
> – Katie Lacz

who's who

Katie Lacz
mother, MDiv,
and spiritual director

What concepts of power are at play in the scripture readings?

What about in your community and neighborhood?

Who is expected to have power and who isn't?

Jesus, Servant of the Lord, empower us in the gifts we bring. Equip us to lead from where we are.

 scripture

Philippians 2:5–11

5 Adopt the attitude that was in Christ Jesus:
6 Though he was in the form of God,
    he did not consider being equal with God something to exploit.
7 But he emptied himself
    by taking the form of a slave
    and by becoming like human beings.
When he found himself in the form of a human, even death on a cross.
9 Therefore, God highly honored him
    and gave him a name above all names,
10   so that at the name of Jesus everyone
    in heaven, on earth, and under the earth might bow
Jesus Christ is Lord, to the glory of God the Father.

Matthew 2: 3–13

3 When King Herod heard this, he was troubled, and everyone in Jerusalem was troubled with him. 4 He gathered all the chief priests and the legal experts and asked them where the Christ was to be born. 5 They said, "In Bethlehem of Judea, for this is what the prophet wrote:
6 You, Bethlehem, land of Judah,
    by no means are you least among the rulers of Judah,
      because from you will come one who governs,
      who will shepherd my people Israel."
7 Then Herod secretly called for the magi and found out from them the time when the star had first appeared. 8 He sent them to Bethlehem, saying, "Go and search carefully for the child. When you've found him, report to me so that I too may go and honor him." 9 When they heard the king, they went; and look, the star they had seen in the east went ahead of them until it stood over the place where the child was. 10 When they saw the star, they were filled with joy. 11 They entered the house and saw the child with Mary his mother. Falling to their knees, they honored him. Then they opened their treasure chests and presented him with gifts of gold, frankincense, and myrrh. 12 Because they were warned in a dream not to return to Herod, they went back to their own country by another route.
13 When the magi had departed, an angel from the Lord appeared to Joseph in a dream and said, "Get up. Take the child and his mother and escape to Egypt. Stay there until I tell you, for Herod will soon search for the child in order to kill him."

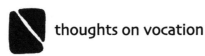 thoughts on vocation

> Socially responsible discernment
> involves **understanding** social structures
> that oppress the poor,
> **asking questions** about how people came to be poor,
> about what makes them poor and keeps them poor.
>
> – John Neafsey

 liturgy of listening

4

Listen, says the Lord God.
Pay attention to my voice.
The sheep know the voice of the shepherd,
This does not necessarily mean the words are clear.
   God desires mercy and not sacrifices,
Temples that shelter and protect the marginalized,
Eventually, the lion shall lie down with the lamb.
Jesus comes not a prince but a pauper,
Stands and sits with sinners,
Shocks the leaders
Shatters expectations.
Stirs up healing and trouble on the Sabbath.
Resurrection and life, ever-defeating death,
Behold, God is on the move.

 who's who

Parker Palmer
author, educator, and activist
Founder and Senior Director of the
Center for Courage & Renewal

going deeper resource

Reading: Amy Tan, "Two Kinds"
A mother and daughter wrestle with expectations and one another. A daughter reflects on their relationship
https://youtu.be/YhT4soKCzNk

Video: TED talk - Ernesto Sirolli "Want to help someone? Shut up and listen!"
Instead of the posture of entering in with the confidence we know how to fix things, Sirolli invites us into the posture of listening, trusting in the capability and wisdom of the people in the midst of the situation, and empowering their own entrepreneurial talents

week 4: listen
thursday: spiritual disciplines

 scripture

Romans 12:15 (NRSV)
Rejoice with those who rejoice, weep with those who weep.

 muévete

Devotional:

> "By the tragic gap I mean the gap between the
> hard realities around us and what we know is possible—
> not because we wish it were so,
> but because we've seen it with our own eyes."
> – Parker J. Palmer

In the news, one doesn't have to look very far to find a tragedy or divisive language, to find a hashtag rallying voices around a cause, to find marginalized and demoralized demographics rising up to speak about their truth and experiences. What trends or stories have especially impacted you, gripped you, kept you up at night? What makes you uncomfortable? What do you do to grieve?

Consider the spiritual practice of bearing witness: from that which we see, we do not look away. With understandable times of rest and a spirit of playfulness mixed in, in what ways can you be intentional about bearing witness?

(Consider this discipline free of shame. While following what breaks your heart, don't beat yourself up if some issues you cannot bear to face. Be kind to yourself and be rooted in grace for yourself and others.)

Spirit of the Living God, may this practice strengthen my spirit and equip me to dwell in your love.

 friday experience

friday experience

before the friday experience

What are you feeling as you head towards this experience?

Expectations? Hopes? Concerns?

Why did you choose this particular Friday Experience?

What questions will you ask?

after the friday experience

4

What justice issues and healing gifts did you notice?

What surprised you about this Experience?

Did you feel energized or depleted while learning about this work?

How might you incorporate what you're learning when you go back home?

Is this a vocation that interests you?

 weekend check-in

No judgment, just noticing. How are you listening to your soul this week?

I was present and fully engaged in muévete ☐

I practiced labyrinth prayer ☐

I practiced external and internal listening ☐

I intentionally thought about my friday experience ☐

What do I want to remember from this week? (write it in this space)

week 4: listen
fifth day: Sabbath rest

 **liturgy of listening**

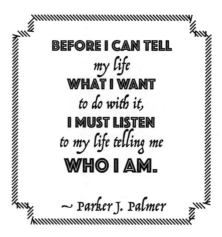 **thoughts on vocation**

Listen, says the Lord God.
Pay attention to my voice.
The sheep know the voice of the shepherd,
This does not necessarily mean the words are clear.
God desires mercy and not sacrifices,
Temples that shelter and protect the marginalized,
Eventually, the lion shall lie down with the lamb.
Jesus comes not a prince but a pauper,
Stands and sits with sinners,
Shocks the leaders
Shatters expectations.
Stirs up healing and trouble on the Sabbath.
Resurrection and life, ever-defeating death,
Behold, God is on the move.

> **BEFORE I CAN TELL**
> *my life*
> **WHAT I WANT**
> *to do with it,*
> **I MUST LISTEN**
> *to my life telling me*
> **WHO I AM.**
>
> ~ *Parker J. Palmer*

 scripture

Psalm 42: 1–6

1 As a deer longs for flowing streams,
  so my soul longs for you, O God.
2 My soul thirsts for God,
  for the living God.
When shall I come and behold
  the face of God?
3 My tears have been my food
  day and night,
while people say to me continually,
  "Where is your God?"

4 These things I remember,
  as I pour out my soul:
how I went with the throng,
  and led them in procession to the house of God,
with glad shouts and songs of thanksgiving,
  a multitude keeping festival.
5 Why are you cast down, O my soul,
  and why are you disquieted within me?
Hope in God; for I shall again praise him,
  my help 6 and my God.

 **muévete**

Devotional:

What have you noticed in listening this week?

What types of vocations or callings are resonating with you?

What does your soul need to enter into rest?

What are you praying for this week?

Good Shepherd, lead me into rest. Lead me beside still waters. On this day, restore my soul.

4

4

4

4

4

4

Liturgy of Presence

(Breathe in) Holy Wisdom
(Breathe out) Guide us.
(Breathe in) Creator God
(Breathe out) Come, Lord Jesus.
May our breathing anchor us in this moment.
The Spirit of God hovers over these waters,
And resides in this place.
Pay attention, for we are standing on holy ground.
Guide us into presence, **may we arrive to the invitation of the moment.**
Guide us into presence, **may we see each other.**
Guide us into presence, **may we encounter the Spirit of God.**

Prayers of the People

For the situations and people that are weighing on our hearts...
...Spirit, carry our prayers.

For the leaders in these communities, and our country....
...Spirit, guide our prayers.

For the systems that promote profit over equality, for the stories we long to find healing, for the demographics that are forgotten or outcast from basic human needs...
...Spirit, help us hold our prayers.

For our part in all this, for our responsibility and opportunity in all this...
...Spirit, help us to see.

God, lead us onward. Make us into the people you call us to be.

Amen.

week

5

presence

week 5: presence
living in balance

 mind

 using your voice

 body

Communication is the backbone and blood of our relationships, but we are often bad at it. We hold in what we should speak. We speak what we regret. We are inconsistent. We don't have the right words. We don't listen to understand.

Miguel Ruiz describes the road to relational peace in his book, "The Four Agreements." He says that if we do two things, we will find peace:

1. **Recognize that everyone is living in their own dream** (reality), and that it is the collision of our personal dreams that create conflict, misunderstanding, and suffering. This means that your mom, best friend, significant other, coworker, stranger, YOU are all operating in a slightly different world based on your own perception of reality that each thinks is THE reality. Practice observing and listening.

2. Make these four agreements to practice in each moment:

- **Be impeccable with your word** (Do what you say you will do.)
- **Always do your best** (Don't take shortcuts or make excuses.)
- **Don't take anything personally** (Don't make what someone else does or says about you. It's about them.)
- **Don't make assumptions** (Don't assume you know what someone else is thinking. Ask them) These two commitments sound simple, but they are profound life-long, daily work.

Most of our miscommunication is based in misunderstanding. How can we be present for each other if we don't understand each other? "They won't know if we don't speak," but we must also "speak the truth in love." There is a tension here that requires listening, silence, wisdom, and practice to understand. It is through contemplation, intention, and practice we find the solid core of our own mind and will, also where we find God's and each other's. This **Spiritual Practice** of Presence will shape your **Relationships** into powerful places to use your voice for healing and creation. Don't let the fear of hurting someone or seeming foolish prevent you from using your voice anymore.

Exercise Five: Speak Your Truth
Speak your truth this week to someone you need to. It could be someone you need to apologize to, a parent or friend that has hurt you but you've never expressed your truth to, or a teacher or mentor who changed your life.
Be very intentional. Carefully think about what you want to say, why you want to say it, how you will say it. Writing this out will be very helpful.
Decide the platform for using your voice: meeting in person, making a phone call, writing a letter or email.
Take time to envision the ideal outcome from sharing your truth. Take time to envision the worst possible outcome. Release the outcome…
…And follow through. Use your voice however you determined.

Reflection: What did it feel like to use your voice to speak your truth?
How did the other person react? How did you react?
How does this change the way you will use your voice moving forward?

week 5: presence
living in balance

 spirit

the practice of being

Lectio divina means "divine reading." It's a Benedictine prayer practice of scripture meditation (you can also use a poem or song lyrics). The text is not an object to be studied but a living word which can speak to your experience, wherever you are at that moment.

Instructions:
Read - slowly read the passage through twice. Notice which words or phrases seem to jump out
Think - think about associations or memories you have around this word or phrase
Pray - talk to God about this memory or feeling
   Where else in my life is this coming up? How shall I respond to this?
   Is God leading me toward or away from something?
Contemplate - let go of all the thoughts and simply be, perhaps focusing just on breathing.

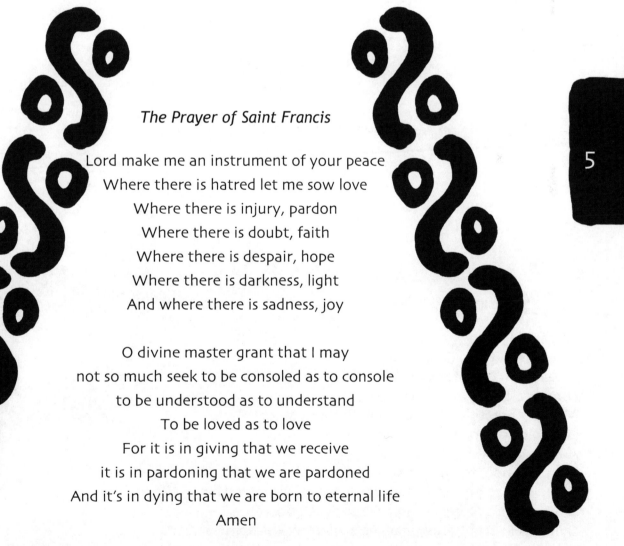

The Prayer of Saint Francis

Lord make me an instrument of your peace
Where there is hatred let me sow love
Where there is injury, pardon
Where there is doubt, faith
Where there is despair, hope
Where there is darkness, light
And where there is sadness, joy

O divine master grant that I may
not so much seek to be consoled as to console
to be understood as to understand
To be loved as to love
For it is in giving that we receive
it is in pardoning that we are pardoned
And it's in dying that we are born to eternal life
Amen

5

week 5: presence
monday: identity formation

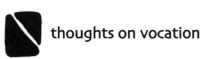 thoughts on vocation

So the burden of what I have to say to you is,

"What is your name—who are you—and can you find a way to hear
the sound of the genuine in yourself?"

There are so many noises going on inside of you,
so many echoes of all sorts,
so many internalizing of the rumble
and the traffic, the confusions,
the disorders by which your environment is peopled

that I wonder if you can get still enough—not quiet enough—still enough
to hear rumbling up
from your unique and essential idiom
the sound of the genuine in you.

– Howard Thurman

ISIS liturgy of presence

 who's who

Malala Yousafzai
education activist and author of
I am Malala: How One Girl Stood Up for
Education and Changed the World

(Breathe in) Holy Wisdom
(Breathe out) Guide us.
(Breathe in) Creator God
(Breathe out) Come, Lord Jesus.
May our breathing anchor us in this moment.
The Spirit of God hovers over these waters,
And resides in this place.
Pay attention, for we are standing on holy ground.
Guide us into presence, **may we arrive to the invitation of the moment.**
Guide us into presence, **may we see each other.**
Guide us into presence, **may we encounter the Spirit of God.**

week 5: presence
monday: identity formation

 scripture

Psalm 94:17–19

17 If the Lord hadn't helped me,
   I would live instantly in total silence.
18 Whenever I feel my foot slipping,
   your faithful love steadies me, Lord.
19 When my anxieties multiply,
   your comforting calms me down.

Psalm 139:13–14

13 You are the one who created my innermost parts;
   you knit me together while I was still in my mother's womb.
14 I give thanks to you that I was marvelously set apart.
   Your works are wonderful—I know that very well.

 muévete

Devotional:

"We human beings don't realize how great God is.
He has given us an extraordinary brain and a sensitive loving heart.
He has blessed us with two lips to talk and express our feelings, two eyes which see a world of colours and beauty, two feet which walk on the road of life, two hands to work for us, and two ears to hear the words of love. As I found with my ear, no one knows how much power they have in their each and every organ until they lose one."
– Malala Yousafzai

"We were scared, but our fear was not as strong as our courage."
– Malala Yousafzai

There are times when, whoever we are, whatever we are capable of, it feels like not enough. When have you felt like you did not have enough to offer a situation?

Take a moment to reflect on the first half of your summer and the work here. Consider the times you have chosen courage over fear. Consider where you have used your brain to understand, your heart to love, your lips to speak, your eyes to see, your feet to move towards someone, your hands to offer assistance, and your ears to listen to another or the sounds around you. You already have so much to offer, right now, right here from where you are standing or sitting.

Creator God, whose image I bear, help me to pay attention to what is occurring within me.

week 5: presence
tuesday: intentional community

 thoughts on vocation

Vocation is not only about "me" and my personal fulfillment,
but about "us" and the common good.
In Buechner's words,

our callings are found
in the places where our "deep gladness"
and the "world's deep hunger" meet,
on the holy ground
where our heart's desire comes together
with what the world most needs from us.

Authentic vocational discernment, therefore, seeks a proper balance
between **inward listening** to our hearts
and **outward, socially engaged listening** with our hearts
to the realities of the world in which we live.

– John Neafsey

 liturgy of presence

(Breathe in) Holy Wisdom
(Breathe out) Guide us.
(Breathe in) Creator God
(Breathe out) Come, Lord Jesus.
May our breathing anchor us in this moment.
The Spirit of God hovers over these waters,
And resides in this place.
Pay attention, for we are standing on holy ground.
Guide us into presence, **may we arrive to the invitation of the moment.**
Guide us into presence, **may we see each other.**
Guide us into presence, **may we encounter the Spirit of God.**

 going deeper resource

Reading: Parker Palmer, "The Gift of Presence"
Palmer writes on being present with people and the healing power of listening to understand
https://onbeing.org/blog/the-gift-of-presence-the-perils-of-advice/

Video: TED talk - Chris Albani "On Humanity"
With a gentle and humorous spirit, Abani shares stories as he models the invitation to reflect humanity back to each other

 **scripture**

Romans 12:9–10

9 Love should be shown without pretending. Hate evil, and hold on to what is good. 10 Love each other like the members of your family. Be the best at showing honor to each other.

1 Kings 19:11–13

11 The Lord said, "Go out and stand at the mountain before the Lord. The Lord is passing by." A very strong wind tore through the mountains and broke apart the stones before the Lord. But the Lord wasn't in the wind. After the wind, there was an earthquake. But the Lord wasn't in the earthquake. 12 After the earthquake, there was a fire. But the Lord wasn't in the fire. After the fire, there was a sound. Thin. Quiet. 13 When Elijah heard it, he wrapped his face in his coat. He went out and stood at the cave's entrance. A voice came to him and said, "Why are you here, Elijah?"

 **muévete**

Devotional:

"We finally learn that we have no 'fix' or 'save' to offer those who suffer deeply.
And yet, we have something better: our gift of self
in the form of personal presence and attention,
the kind that invites the other's soul to show up."
– Parker Palmer

When have you felt deeply and fully heard in your life?

Who do you know that listens well?

What do you feel when someone is paying full attention (not on their phone, distracted, or even giving advice or telling a story about themselves in response)?

Who needs your presence and attentiveness this week?

Whose soul needs the invitation of our presence to show up?

Community of Love, Parent, Son, and Holy Spirit, teach me to see your image in my brother, sister, enemy, friend, and neighbor.

week 5: presence
wednesday: servant leadership

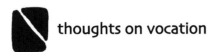 thoughts on vocation

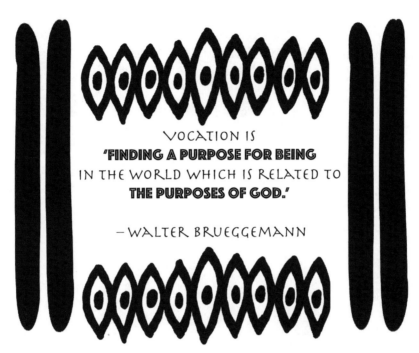

VOCATION IS
'FINDING A PURPOSE FOR BEING
IN THE WORLD WHICH IS RELATED TO
THE PURPOSES OF GOD.'

—WALTER BRUEGGEMANN

5

muévete

Devotional:

"The human soul doesn't want to be advised or fixed or saved.
It simply wants to be witnessed—to be seen, heard and companioned exactly as it is.
When we make that kind of deep bow to the soul of a suffering person,
our respect reinforces the soul's healing resources,
the only resources that can help the sufferer make it through."
– Parker Palmer, from "The Gift of Presence, the Perils of Advice"

It can be difficult to be present if we don't believe we have much to offer.

And yet, leading by simply being present to someone—not giving advice or fixing—empowers another to access their own resources. With this posture of service, each person can begin to know they have within them tools and wisdom to trust. We become empowered, capable, resilient beings, all arriving to the communal table to offer our wisdom, share our gifts, and witness the dignity and humanity and divinity in each other.

Jesus, Servant of the Lord, empower us in the gifts we bring. Equip us to lead from where we are.

 **scripture**

Colossians 1:15–17

15 The Son is the image of the invisible God,
    the one who is first over all creation,
16 Because all things were created by him:
    both in the heavens and on the earth,
    the things that are visible and the things that are invisible.
      Whether they are thrones or powers,
      or rulers or authorities,
    all things were created through him and for him.
17 He existed before all things,
    and all things are held together in him.

John 1:1–3

1 In the beginning was the Word
   and the Word was with God
   and the Word was God.
2 The Word was with God in the beginning.
3 Everything came into being through the Word,
   and without the Word
   nothing came into being.
What came into being

5

liturgy of presence

(Breathe in) Holy Wisdom
(Breathe out) Guide us.
(Breathe in) Creator God
(Breathe out) Come, Lord Jesus.
May our breathing anchor us in this moment.
The Spirit of God hovers over these waters,
And resides in this place.
Pay attention, for we are standing on holy ground.
Guide us into presence, **may we arrive to the invitation of the moment.**
Guide us into presence, **may we see each other.**
Guide us into presence, **may we encounter the Spirit of God.**

week 5: presence
thursday: spiritual disciplines

 thoughts on vocation

Discovering vocation
does *not* mean scrambling
toward some prize just
beyond my reach
but
accepting the treasure of true self
I already possess.

Vocation
does not come from a voice **out there**
calling me to be something I am not.
It *comes from* a voice **in here**
calling me to
be the person I was born to be,
to fulfill the original selfhood
given me at birth by God.

– Thomas Merton

When it is genuine,
when it is born of the need to speak,
no one can stop the human voice.
When denied a mouth,
it speaks with the hands or the eyes,
or the pores, or anything at all.
Because every single one of us
has something to say to the others,
something that deserves
to be celebrated or forgiven by others.

– Eduardo Galeano

muévete

Devotional:
Watch the four minute TED Talk: Clint Smith, "The Danger of Silence"

"We spend so much time listening to the things people are saying
that we rarely pay attention to the things they don't.
Silence is the residue of fear.
It is feeling your flaws gut-wrench guillotine your tongue. It is the air retreating
from your chest because it doesn't feel safe in your lungs.
Silence is Rwandan genocide. Silence is Katrina.
It is what you hear when there aren't enough body bags left. It is the sound
after the noose is already tied. It is charring. It is chains. It is privilege. It is pain.
There is no time to pick your battles when your battles have already picked you.
I will not let silence wrap itself around my indecision."
– Clint Smith

Where do you struggle to speak up or use your voice? Where and with whom do you feel more comfortable in your voice? Does your voice feel powerful, powerless, or somewhere in between? What would practicing the discipline of using your voice look like in your work and life?

Spirit of the Living God, may this practice strengthen my spirit and equip me to dwell in your love.

week 5: presence
thursday: spiritual disciplines

 **scripture**

2 Kings 20:5
Turn around. Say to Hezekiah, my people's leader: This is what the Lord, the God of your ancestor David, says: I have heard your prayer and have seen your tears. So now I'm going to heal you. Three days from now you will be able to go up to the Lord's temple.

Exodus 3:7
Then the Lord said, "I've clearly seen my people oppressed in Egypt. I've heard their cry of injustice because of their slave masters. I know about their pain.

Esther 4:14
In fact, if you don't speak up at this very important time, relief and rescue will appear for the Jews from another place, but you and your family will die. But who knows? Maybe it was for a moment like this that you came to be part of the royal family.

spiritual discipline: using your voice

5

liturgy of presence

(Breathe in) Holy Wisdom
(Breathe out) Guide us.
(Breathe in) Creator God
(Breathe out) Come, Lord Jesus.
May our breathing anchor us in this moment.
The Spirit of God hovers over these waters,
And resides in this place.
Pay attention, for we are standing on holy ground.
Guide us into presence, **may we arrive to the invitation of the moment.**
Guide us into presence, **may we see each other.**
Guide us into presence, **may we encounter the Spirit of God.**

 who's who

Clint Smith
writer and teacher
doctoral candidate at Harvard studying
education, incarceration, and inequality

week 5: presence
friday experience

 friday experience

before the friday experience

What are you feeling as you head towards this experience?

Expectations? Hopes? Concerns?

Why did you choose this particular Friday Experience?

What questions will you ask?

after the friday experience

What justice issues and healing gifts did you notice?

What surprised you about this Experience?

Did you feel energized or depleted while learning about this work?

How might you incorporate what you're learning when you go back home?

Is this a vocation that interests you?

5

 weekend check-in

No judgment, just noticing. How are you listening to your soul this week?

I was present and fully engaged in muévete ☐

I practiced lectio divina ☐

I spoke my truth ☐

I intentionally thought about my friday experience ☐

What do I want to remember from this week? (write it in this space)

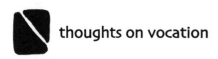 **thoughts on vocation**

> **From the beginning,
> our lives lay down clues
> to selfhood and vocation,
> though the clues may be
> hard to decode.
> But trying to interpret them
> is profoundly worthwhile.**
>
> **- Parker Palmer**

 liturgy of presence

(Breathe in) Holy Wisdom
(Breathe out) Guide us.
(Breathe in) Creator God
(Breathe out) Come, Lord Jesus.
May our breathing anchor us in this moment.
The Spirit of God hovers over these waters,
And resides in this place.
Pay attention, for we are standing on holy ground.
Guide us into presence, **may we arrive to the invitation of the moment.**
Guide us into presence, **may we see each other.**
Guide us into presence, **may we encounter the Spirit of God.**

muévete

Devotional:
How have you been present this week?

What types of vocations or callings are resonating with you?

What does your soul need to enter into rest?

What are you praying for this week?

Good Shepherd, lead me into rest. Lead me beside still waters. On this day, restore my soul.

5

5

5

5

5

5

Liturgy of Release

The pilgrim puts feet to road,
trusting that the God who led the Israelites through the desert will guide by flame and cloud.
The lilies dance and bloom,
trusting that the God who planted them will give nourishment.
Fear teaches us to run,
Courage invites us to speak.
Shame teaches us to hide,
Love invites us to dance.
Remove our lights from under their shades
Embrace our part of the whole
Stand up and alongside each other
Rest knowing that we are all in this together.
Be the body Christ invites us to be.
Release.
We are all in this together.

Prayers of the People

For the expectations we are invited to release, of ourselves, each other, and other people…
…God, help us to see as you see.

For the places we find security and the ways we are led into the unknown…
…God, guide us by your light and lead our feet.

For the stereotypes and judgments we hold to, and the ways that blind us from seeing in wholeness…
…God, help us to see as you see.

For the invitations each day that draw us into your Love and compassion…
…Spirit, teach us not to fear where you guide us.

For the systems we benefit from that leave some out of the equation,
For the ways we are culpable in systems of injustice…
…God, forgive us. Help us to be part of the healing.

Amen.

week
6
release

A New Creed (1968) from the United Church of Canada:

We are not alone,
    we live in God's world.
We believe in God:
    who has created and is creating,
    who has come in Jesus,
      the Word made flesh,
      to reconcile and make new,
    who works in us and others
      by the Spirit.
We trust in God.
We are called to be the Church:
    to celebrate God's presence,
    to live with respect in Creation,
    to love and serve others,
    to seek justice and resist evil,
    to proclaim Jesus, crucified and risen,
      our judge and our hope.
In life, in death, in life beyond death,
    God is with us.
We are not alone.
Thanks be to God.

week 6: release
living in balance

 mind

share power

"Be content with what you have;
rejoice in the way things are.
When you realize there is nothing lacking,
the whole world belongs to you."
Lao Tzu

 body

We often define power by things we have: prestige, success, wealth, scholastic accolades, beauty. The logical trajectory, then, of growing personal power becomes a path of acquisition. How bizarre, then, to hear Christ say things like, "Give everything you have to the poor and follow me...be the least on earth and in this you will be greatest in heaven." This seems to be what we are striving to get away from, right? Being poor, simple, anonymous.

Ancient religions, such as Taoism and Buddhism, reflect the words of Christ, naming Non-Attachment and "letting go" as a sign of premier spiritual strength. Non-Attachment does not mean you do not care about things. It means your primary devotion is to something much larger: community collaboration vs. independent competition. Your primary posture is humbly open-handed vs. clenched fists grasping what they have. It is trust vs. control. This is the pearl of true power.

Letting go creates a container of possibility. It risks the present for the possible. This requires deep faith. It also requires us to rely on others, to work together, to share. This is harder work than controlling your own life. It's easier to go cheap for your own personal power, but this means YOU are the cap of potential. Sharing power exponentially broadens the collective potential of power in the world. We gain the power of the world through the **Spiritual Practice** of releasing purely personal power by sharing power through **Relationship.**

Exercise Six: Letting Go
Begin the practice of sharing power by releasing something you don't need this week.
There are myriad ways to learn the practice of release, BUT, the simplest practice is releasing things. This is the gateway to greater spiritual release.

Challenge:
Go through the things you have in your room.
Ask yourself two questions for each item: Do I need this item? Does this item spark joy?
If the answer to both of those questions is "Yes," keep it. If it isn't, donate it. Commit to donating at least one item you have.
Hold and thank each item you choose to release and pray it brings joy or usefulness to someone. (This will feel very silly.)
(Exercise adapted from the work of Marie Kondo in "The Life-Changing Magic of Tidying Up")

Reflection: How does it feel to release something you weren't planning to?

6

week 6: release
living in balance

 spirit

the practice of creativity and imagination

Gospel Imagination is a prayer form through which you imagine yourself as a character in the story in order to reflect on the gospel passage. While reading the passage, use all your senses—hearing, seeing, touching, smelling, and tasting—to bring the story alive. Let go of any anxiety over historical accuracy and allow your imagination to play with the story. Our purpose in this prayer is not realism, but to investigate the humanness of Jesus and the other characters, to think about how we might respond to what's going on in the story, and to ground the story in our own embodied experience.

Instructions:
Using the gospel text below, read through the story once or twice to be familiar with the basic story. Set the text aside and reconstruct the story in your mind, adding yourself into the narrative. What is this environment like? Is it hot or cold? What do you hear, see and smell?
What's going on as people in the story interact and respond to what is said? What emotions do you sense in yourself? How are you related to the other characters? Are you near or far?
Imagine a conversation between yourself and another character. What is said? How does it feel? Write your story in the journaling pages.

Matthew 20:1–16 (Common English Bible)

Jesus is speaking this parable:

"The kingdom of heaven is like a landowner who went out early in the morning to hire workers for his vineyard. After he agreed with the workers to pay them a denarion, he sent them into his vineyard.
"Then he went out around nine in the morning and saw others standing around the marketplace doing nothing. He said to them, 'You also go into the vineyard, and I'll pay you whatever is right.' And they went.
"Again around noon and then at three in the afternoon, he did the same thing. Around five in the afternoon he went and found others standing around, and he said to them, 'Why are you just standing around here doing nothing all day long?'
"'Because nobody has hired us,' they replied.
"He responded, 'You also go into the vineyard.'
"When evening came, the owner of the vineyard said to his manager, 'Call the workers and give them their wages, beginning with the last ones hired and moving on finally to the first.' When those who were hired at five in the afternoon came, each one received a denarion. Now when those hired first came, they thought they would receive more. But each of them also received a denarion. When they received it, they grumbled against the landowner, 'These who were hired last worked one hour, and they received the same pay as we did even though we had to work the whole day in the hot sun.'
"But he replied to one of them, 'Friend, I did you no wrong. Didn't I agree to pay you a denarion? Take what belongs to you and go. I want to give to this one who was hired last the same as I give to you. Don't I have the right to do what I want with what belongs to me? Or are you resentful because I'm generous?' So those who are last will be first. And those who are first will be last."

6

week 6: release
monday: identity formation

 **muévete**

Devotional:

"Camas Lilies" by Lynn Ungar

"Consider the lilies of the field,
the blue banks of camas opening
into acres of sky along the road.
Would the longing to lie down
and be washed by that beauty
abate if you knew their usefulness,
how the native ground their bulbs
for flour, how the settlers' hogs
uprooted them, grunting in gleeful
oblivion as the flowers fell?

And you—what of your rushed
and useful life? Imagine setting it all down—
papers, plans, appointments, everything—
leaving only a note: 'Gone
to the fields to be lovely. Be back
when I'm through blooming.'

Even now, unneeded and uneaten,
the camas lilies gaze out above the grass
from their tender blue eyes.
Even in sleep your life will shine.
Make no mistake. Of course
your work will always matter.
Yet Solomon in all his glory
was not arrayed like one of these."

6

 thoughts on vocation

A vocation entails
making ourselves **available**
to something **good.**
It reminds us that **to be human**
is to want **our lives to count**
for something **worthwhile,**

while to live
only for our own gratification
depletes us.

Regardless of its **duration**
or **depth or significance,**
every calling of our lives
is a summons **to fully inhabit**
our best selves—**to become**
the people that we ought to be.
Perhaps surprisingly,
we become **most fully ourselves**
when we focus, not on ourselves
(through lives of careful calculation
and strategic self-promotion),
but on something **greater than ourselves.**

- Paul J. Wadell

 who's who

Lynn Ungar
author of
Bread and Other Miracles
www.lynnungar.com

A display like Solomon's could make anyone feel safe in society. Plenty in savings, a great spot in the local neighborhood, plenty to wear no matter what the occasion, and never a shortage of food. And yet, we are invited to trust not in the structure of stockpiling, but in the providence of God.

What does this concept of trust bring to your mind?

How are you blooming in this experience?

What are you releasing in that process?

Creator God, whose image I bear, help me to pay attention to what is occurring within me.

week 6: release
monday: identity formation

 scripture

1 Kings 10:4–9, 23–26
4 When the queen of Sheba saw how wise Solomon was, the palace he had built, 5 the food on his table, the servants' quarters, the function and dress of his attendants, his cupbearers, and the entirely burned offerings that he offered at the Lord's temple, it took her breath away.
6 "The report I heard about your deeds and wisdom when I was still at home is true," she said to the king. 7 "I didn't believe it until I came and saw it with my own eyes. In fact, the half of it wasn't even told to me! You have far more wisdom and wealth than I was told. 8 Your people and these servants who continually serve you and get to listen to your wisdom are truly happy! 9 Bless the Lord your God because he was pleased to place you on Israel's throne. Because the Lord loved Israel with an eternal love, the Lord made you king to uphold justice and righteousness."

23 King Solomon far exceeded all the earth's kings in wealth and wisdom, 24 and so the whole earth wanted an audience with Solomon in order to hear his God-given wisdom. 25 Year after year they came with tribute: objects of silver and gold, clothing, weapons, spices, horses, and mules.
26 Solomon acquired more and more chariots and horses until he had fourteen hundred chariots and twelve thousand horses that he kept in chariot cities and with the king in Jerusalem.

Matthew 6:26–30
26 Look at the birds in the sky. They don't sow seed or harvest grain or gather crops into barns. Yet your heavenly Father feeds them. Aren't you worth much more than they are? 27 Who among you by worrying can add a single moment to your life? 28 And why do you worry about clothes? Notice how the lilies in the field grow. They don't wear themselves out with work, and they don't spin cloth. 29 But I say to you that even Solomon in all of his splendor wasn't dressed like one of these. 30 If God dresses grass in the field so beautifully, even though it's alive today and tomorrow it's thrown into the furnace, won't God do much more for you, you people of weak faith?

liturgy of release

The pilgrim puts feet to road,
trusting that the God who led the Israelites through the desert
will guide by flame and cloud.
The lilies dance and bloom,
trusting that the God who planted them will give nourishment.
Fear teaches us to run,
Courage invites us to speak.
Shame teaches us to hide,
Love invites us to dance.
Remove our lights from under their shades
Embrace our part of the whole
Stand up and alongside each other
Rest knowing that we are all in this together.
Be the body Christ invites us to be.
Release.
We are all in this together.

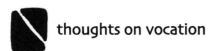 **thoughts on vocation**

*The sense of vocation
arises at the point
where a* **crying need,
a call,
an appeal**
*seems to be addressed to us
that we can only answer
by sharing the* **endowments,
talents,
and skills**
we have been given.

– Sam Keen

who's who

Maya Angelou
American poet, singer memorist, and civil rights activist

 muévete

Devotional:

"Let nothing dim the light that shines from within."
– Maya Angelou

As you may have already encountered, community can be a challenge. Differences can become frustrating, tensions can rise. But as a body, there is benefit to having noses and ears and eyes and elbows rather than all sharing the same functions.

6

In improv comedy, one of the foundational rules is liking each other. Instead of one person being the star of the show, the best improvisational skits are when all are co-creating together, arriving with a "yes, and…" This involves trusting each other and releasing the (expected) outcome.

What can emerge when everyone is showing up with their gifts and co-creating?

In what ways have you seen light and gifts shine from the people around you?

What light and gifts do you offer?

How can you encourage and support the people around you?

Community of Love, Parent, Son, and Holy Spirit, teach me to see your image in my brother, sister, enemy, friend, and neighbor.

 scripture

Matthew 5:14–16

14 You are the light of the world. A city on top of a hill can't be hidden. 15 Neither do people light a lamp and put it under a basket. Instead, they put it on top of a lampstand, and it shines on all who are in the house. 16 In the same way, let your light shine before people, so they can see the good things you do and praise your Father who is in heaven.

1 Corinthians 12:4–7, 11–13, 24b–27

4 There are different spiritual gifts but the same Spirit; 5 and there are different ministries and the same Lord; 6 and there are different activities but the same God who produces all of them in everyone. 7 A demonstration of the Spirit is given to each person for the common good.

11 All these things are produced by the one and same Spirit who gives what he wants to each person. 12 Christ is just like the human body—a body is a unit and has many parts; and all the parts of the body are one body, even though there are many. 13 We were all baptized by one Spirit into one body, whether Jew or Greek, or slave or free, and we all were given one Spirit to drink. 14 Certainly the body isn't one part but many.

24b But God has put the body together, giving greater honor to the part with less honor 25 so that there won't be division in the body and so the parts might have mutual concern for each other. 26 If one part suffers, all the parts suffer with it; if one part gets the glory, all the parts celebrate with it. 27 You are the body of Christ and parts of each other.

liturgy of release

The pilgrim puts feet to road,
trusting that the God who led the Israelites through the desert
will guide by flame and cloud.
The lilies dance and bloom,
trusting that the God who planted them will give nourishment.
Fear teaches us to run,
Courage invites us to speak.
Shame teaches us to hide,
Love invites us to dance.
Remove our lights from under their shades
Embrace our part of the whole
Stand up and alongside each other
Rest knowing that we are all in this together.
Be the body Christ invites us to be.
Release.
We are all in this together.

6

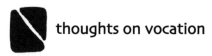 thoughts on vocation

THERE ARE
ALL DIFFERENT KINDS OF VOICES
CALLING YOU...
AND THE PROBLEM IS
to find out
WHICH IS THE VOICE OF GOD
RATHER THAN
OF **Society,** SAY,
OR **the Superego,**
OR **Self-Interest.**

– FREDERICK BUECHNER

What keeps me going?
Well, it's like a **fire**...
a consuming, **nagging,**
every day and every-moment
demand of my soul
to just do it.
It's difficult to explain.
I like to think
it's the good Spirit
asking me to do it.
I hope so...
If you really want something
you have to sacrifice.
Because of my **faith**
the concept of **sacrifice**
is understood.

– Cesar Chavez

 liturgy of release

6

The pilgrim puts feet to road,
trusting that the God who led the Israelites through the desert
will guide by flame and cloud.
The lilies dance and bloom,
trusting that the God who planted them will give nourishment.
Fear teaches us to run,
Courage invites us to speak.
Shame teaches us to hide,
Love invites us to dance.
Remove our lights from under their shades
Embrace our part of the whole
Stand up and alongside each other
Rest knowing that we are all in this together.
Be the body Christ invites us to be.
Release.
We are all in this together.

week 6: release
wednesday: servant leadership

 scripture

Philippians 3:8–10

8 But even beyond that, I consider everything a loss in comparison with the superior value of knowing Christ Jesus my Lord. I have lost everything for him, but what I lost I think of as sewer trash, so that I might gain Christ 9 and be found in him. In Christ I have a righteousness that is not my own and that does not come from the Law but rather from the faithfulness of Christ. It is the righteousness of God that is based on faith. 10 The righteousness that I have comes from knowing Christ, the power of his resurrection, and the participation in his sufferings. It includes being conformed to his death.

 going deeper resource

Video: TED talk - Chimamanda Ngozi Adichie, "The danger of a single story"
What do we risk and lose if we only entertain one story?

 muévete

Devotional:
"[The Examen] questions help us identify moments of consolation and desolation. For centuries prayerful people have found direction for their day and for their life by identifying these moments." (Sleeping With Bread, Linn, Linn, & Linn, 3)

The prayer of Examen is an Ignatian practice of identifying and discerning that which we are called to, and that which is draining to our lives and work. They are a powerful tool for discovering how God is leading in our lives.

Consider the following questions:

When did you feel most alive this week?
When did you most feel life draining out of you?

When did you give and receive the most love this week?
When did you give and receive the least love this week?

Jesus, Servant of the Lord, empower us in the gifts we bring. Equip us to lead from where we are.

6

week 6: release
thursday: spiritual disciplines

 thoughts on vocation

So many
of the vocational discernment texts and practices
have turned us inward,
to look at ourselves
            or "whole selves,"
without understanding that our whole selves
include our elders,
            ancestors,
                        and our communities.
A narrative approach to Christian vocation
shows how narratives are intergenerational
and are a connection
            between the living and the dead.

– Dr. Patrick Reyes

 muévete

Devotional:

"You don't need to be a voice for the voiceless. Just pass the mic."
– Su'ad Abdul Khabeer

6

Have you ever experienced your voice silenced?

Where do you see voices left out or disempowered in the community? Where do you see this back home?

What platforms are available to you where you could lift up someone else's voice?

Do you know anyone who models this well?

Spirit of the Living God, may this practice strengthen my spirit and equip me to dwell in your love.

week 6: release
thursday: spiritual disciplines

 scripture

Psalm 31:8–9

8 You didn't hand me over to the enemy,
   but set my feet in wide-open spaces.
9 Have mercy on me, Lord, because I'm depressed.
   My vision fails because of my grief,
   as do my spirit and my body.

spiritual discipline:
share power

who's who

Su'ad Abdul Khabeer
scholar-artist activist
who uses anthropology
and performance
to explore the intersections of
race and popular culture

6

IEIE liturgy of release

The pilgrim puts feet to road,
**trusting that the God who led the Israelites through the desert
will guide by flame and cloud.**
The lilies dance and bloom,
trusting that the God who planted them will give nourishment.
Fear teaches us to run,
Courage invites us to speak.
Shame teaches us to hide,
Love invites us to dance.
Remove our lights from under their shades
Embrace our part of the whole
Stand up and alongside each other
Rest knowing that we are all in this together.
Be the body Christ invites us to be.
Release.
We are all in this together.

week 6: release
friday experience

 friday experience

before the friday experience

What are you feeling as you head towards this experience?

Expectations? Hopes? Concerns?

Why did you choose this particular Friday Experience?

What questions will you ask?

after the friday experience

What justice issues and healing gifts did you notice?

What surprised you about this Experience?

Did you feel energized or depleted while learning about this work?

How might you incorporate what you're learning wehn you go back home?

Is this a vocation that interests you?

weekend check-in

6

No judgment, just noticing. How are you listening to your soul this week?

I was present and fully engaged in muévete ☐

I practiced gospel imagination prayer ☐

I let go of _____ ☐

I intentionally thought about my friday experience ☐

What do I want to remember from this week? (write it in this space)

week 6: release
fifth day: Sabbath rest

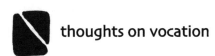 thoughts on vocation

liturgy of release

The pilgrim puts feet to road,
trusting that the God who led the Israelites through the desert will guide by flame and cloud.
The lilies dance and bloom,
trusting that the God who planted them will give nourishment.
Fear teaches us to run,
Courage invites us to speak.
Shame teaches us to hide,
Love invites us to dance.
Remove our lights from under their shades
Embrace our part of the whole
Stand up and alongside each other
Rest knowing that we are all in this together.
Be the body Christ invites us to be.
Release.
We are all in this together.

 scripture

Psalm 121
I raise my eyes toward the mountains.
    Where will my help come from?
2 My help comes from the Lord,
    the maker of heaven and earth.
3 God won't let your foot slip.
    Your protector won't fall asleep on the job.
4 No! Israel's protector
    never sleeps or rests!
5 The Lord is your protector;
    the Lord is your shade right beside you.
6 The sun won't strike you during the day;
    neither will the moon at night.
7 The Lord will protect you from all evil;
    God will protect your very life.
8 The Lord will protect you on your journeys
    whether going or coming—
    from now until forever from now.

6

 muévete

Devotional:
What have you been releasing this week?

What has been difficult to release?

What types of vocations or callings are resonating with you?

What does your soul need to enter into rest?

What are you praying for this week?

Good Shepherd, lead me into rest. Lead me beside still waters. On this day, restore my soul.

6

6

6

week 6: release
journaling pages

6

6

6

Liturgy of Bringing

What do we carry from this place?
What have we gathered that needs to be shared?
Our lives, as Christ's, become an offering.
Our stories are ours, and they are also for the greater whole of the community.
We bring our collective wisdom and God-sightings to the table,
Together, we piece together a holy puzzle.
Reveal to us the justice that will emerge from our hands and feet,
Show us the opportunities to bring healing and hope with our words and our presence,
Teach us the story of Love and how to tell it.
Introduce us to one another again and again,
We belong to one another.
Let's tell everyone they're already in the Imago Dei.

Prayers of the People

God, what do we take from this experience?
…Spirit, illuminate for us our next steps.

God, what has changed for and within us in this experience?
…Spirit, guide us.

God, who have we encountered that we will not easily forget?
…Jesus, help us to follow your footsteps.

What is next for us in our lives as we discern and seek to live in the reign of God?
…Spirit, lead us on.

May the ones who need us be clear.
May the God who guides us be present.
May the work ahead of us be done in community.
May we always have your Spirit to guide us.
Amen.

week

7

bring

week 7: bring living in balance

 mind

preaching love

 body

What is love? We all want it and search for it.
Most songs and stories are written about it. But what is it?

The mystery of love is that it cannot be concretely be defined or held on to. We can see examples and objects of love, but, really, it is this invisible, incredibly powerful force that seems like wind or magic.

> **WORK**
> **is love**
> **MADE VISIBLE.**
>
> Khalil Gibran
> "The Prophet"

Christ says the entire scripture is fulfilled "By loving God and loving our neighbor as our self." Wow. This, then, is our highest aim. It's difficult to love everyone all the time, it would really be a super-human accomplishment. But that's the thing. It's not an accomplishment. You can't arrive to a new level like a graduation or video game. Love is a continual ebb and flow, where we constantly stay the course to expand our capacity to love. Love is in action, moment by moment. It is a constant meditation. Lao Tzu says, " A journey of a thousand miles begins in a single step." It's millions of single steps that enable us to be love, to be the hands and feet of God.

Each thought, word, and action builds something. "Whatever we feed grows." We need to examine what we are creating each day. We have the choice to feed love or feed hate/self-centeredness/indifference with every choice we make.

Learning to love looks like the **Physical Activity** of choosing kindness each moment. This is the true, eternal essence of **Meaningful Work.**

Exercise Seven: Daily Kindness

- *Do something unnecessarily kind each day this week, something you wouldn't normally take time to do.* This could be something as simple as encouraging someone who looks sad, doubly tipping a waitress, giving a small gift to brighten someone's day, calling your mom because you know it will make her smile, volunteering to do something you don't have to do.
  - Get a single piece of paper. Write a short paragraph about your intentional act of kindness each day. By the end of the week, you will have seven acts.
  - Say a prayer each day: "God, thank you for the ability to grow love by being your hands and feet today. Give me eyes to see. Shape my mind in Your Creativity and Living Love."

7

Reflection: How did being intentional about demonstrating daily kindness affect your powers of observation or your perspective of situations?

What is your overall reaction to choosing kindness as a practice?

How could this change our communities?

week 7: bring
living in balance

 spirit

the practice of praying for others

String prayer is a pocket-handy prayer method of praying for others. Tie five evenly spaced knots in a piece of string. You could include a bead in each knot and a small symbol such as a cross or peace sign at one end as the starting knot. With your knotted string, you are ready to begin the prayer. You may choose to use the formal liturgical words below or your own words for each knot.

Instructions:
Preparation - Take a few deep breaths. Hold the first knot (or symbol) in your fingers and repeat a word such as "Peace" or "Love" several times.

A (adoration) - Move to the second knot and say a prayer of praise:
"Glory be to God and to Jesus and to the Holy Spirit.
As it was in the beginning, is now and will be forever and ever."

C (confession) - Move to the third knot and say a prayer of confession:
"I confess that I have not loved you with my whole heart. I have not loved my neighbor, and I have not cared for the Earth. Forgive me and free me from spiritual blindness and self-centered living."

T (thanksgiving) - Move to the fourth knot and say a prayer of thanksgiving:
"I give thanks to you, Creator of heaven and earth."

S (supplication) - Move to the fifth knot and say prayers of petition, which means to ask for something, whatever you need at this time.
"With bread we need for today, feed us.
For the hurts we absorb from one another, comfort us.
In times of temptation and test, strengthen us.
From trials too great to endure, spare us.
From the grip of all that is evil, free us."

To continue in intercessory prayer, begin at this fifth knot and work back toward the beginning of the string.

Fifth knot (S): pray for a specific person you know is in need

Fourth knot (T): pray for a specific person to whom you are thankful

Third knot (C): pray for a specific person you have hurt and need to ask for forgiveness from

Second knot (A): Pray for a specific person you love dearly

First knot (or symbol): end your prayer with the same word you repeated at the beginning.

7

week 7: bring
monday: identity formation

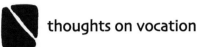 thoughts on vocation

[**Work**] is, or it should be,
the full expression of the workers' **gifts,**
the thing in which he finds **spiritual,**
mental
and **bodily satisfaction,**
and the **medium** in which he offers himself to God.

- **Dorothy Sayers**

 liturgy of bringing

What do we carry from this place?
What have we gathered that needs to be shared?
Our lives, as Christ's, become an offering.
Our stories are ours, and they are also for the greater whole of the community.
We bring our collective wisdom and God-sightings to the table,
Together, we piece together a holy puzzle.
Reveal to us the justice that will emerge from our hands and feet,
Show us the opportunities to bring healing and hope with our words and our presence,
Teach us the story of Love and how to tell it.
Introduce us to one another again and again,
We belong to one another.
Let's tell everyone they're already in the Imago Dei.

7

going deeper resource

Video: TED talk - Emilie Wapnick, "Why some of us don't have one true calling"
Maybe being one thing when you grow up is a myth. Enter the multipotentialite.

week 7: bring
monday: identity formation

 **scripture**

Matthew 4:19–20

19 "Come, follow me," he said, "and I'll show you how to fish for people." 20 Right away, they left their nets and followed him.

who's who
Melissa Harris-Perry
American writer, professor, television host and political commentator with a focus on African American politics

 **muévete**

Devotional:

"[Sisters] are more than the sum of their relative disadvantages:
they are active agents who craft meaning out of their circumstances
and do so in complicated and diverse ways."
– Melissa Harris-Perry

"The true meaning of life is to plant trees
under whose shade you do not expect to sit."
– Wesley Henderson, writer

As part of a whole, it is important to both cultivate and construct meaning from our own circumstances, and also to cultivate and construct meaning on behalf and for the benefit of the wider community. These go hand in hand and inform one another. Who we are and what we have is never only about us. What serves and nurtures the community also serves and nurtures our own well-being.

What comes to mind when you read these two quotes?

What wisdom will you bring back home with you from this summer experience?

Creator God, whose image I bear, help me to pay attention to what is occurring within me.

7

 thoughts on vocation

WHAT MATTERS
is that the world
should touch
THE HEART
and that the heart
should go out
TOWARDS THE WORLD.

– Jose Garcia

 muévete

Devotional:

"The philosophy of Ubuntu derives from a Nguni word, ubuntu meaning 'the quality of being human.' Ubuntu manifests itself through various human acts, clearly visible in social, political, and economic situations, as well as among family. According to sociolinguist Buntu Mfenyana, it 'runs through the veins of all Africans, is embodied in the oft-repeated: 'Ubuntu ngumtu ngabanye abantu' ('A person is a person through other people'). This African proverb reveals a world view that we owe our selfhood to others, that we are first and foremost social beings, that, if you will, no man/woman is an island, or as the African would have it, 'One finger cannot pick up a grain.' Ubuntu is, at the same time, a deeply personal philosophy that calls on us to mirror our humanity for each other."
– Rev. William E. Flippin, Jr., church planter and grassroots strategist

"[Wakanda] will no longer watch from the shadows. We can not. We must not. We will work to be an example of how we, as brothers and sisters on this earth, should treat each other. Now, more than ever, the illusions of division threaten our very existence. We all know the truth: more connects us than separates us. But in times of crisis the wise build bridges, while the foolish build barriers. We must find a way to look after one another, as if we were one single tribe."
– T'Challa, 2018 movie Black Panther

7

What are some ways you have together built bridges this summer?

Where have you seen Ubuntu embodied?

Community of Love, Parent, Son, and Holy Spirit, teach me to see your image in my brother, sister, enemy, friend, and neighbor.

week 7: bring
tuesday: intentional community

 scripture

Genesis 12:1–3
The Lord said to Abram, "Leave your land, your family, and your father's household for the land that I will show you. 2 I will make of you a great nation and will bless you. I will make your name respected, and you will be a blessing.
3 I will bless those who bless you,
  those who curse you I will curse;
    all the families of the earth
      will be blessed because of you."

Genesis 1:26–27
Then God said, "Let us make humanity in our image to resemble us so that they may take charge of the fish of the sea, the birds in the sky, the livestock, all the earth, and all the crawling things on earth."
27 God created humanity in God's own image,
  in the divine image God created them.

KIK liturgy of bringing

What do we carry from this place?
What have we gathered that needs to be shared?
Our lives, as Christ's, become an offering.
Our stories are ours, and they are also for the greater whole of the community.
We bring our collective wisdom and God-sightings to the table,
Together, we piece together a holy puzzle.
Reveal to us the justice that will emerge from our hands and feet,
Show us the opportunities to bring healing and hope with our words and our presence,
Teach us the story of Love and how to tell it.
Introduce us to one another again and again,
We belong to one another.
Let's tell everyone they're already in the Imago Dei.

week 7: bring
wednesday: servant leadership

 thoughts on vocation

*A career seeks to be successful,
a calling to be valuable.
A career tries to make money,
a calling tries to make a difference.*

– William Sloane Coffin

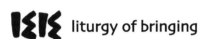 liturgy of bringing

What do we carry from this place?
What have we gathered that needs to be shared?
Our lives, as Christ's, become an offering.
Our stories are ours, and they are also for the greater whole of the community.
We bring our collective wisdom and God-sightings to the table,
Together, we piece together a holy puzzle.
Reveal to us the justice that will emerge from our hands and feet,
Show us the opportunities to bring healing and hope with our words and our presence,
Teach us the story of Love and how to tell it.
Introduce us to one another again and again,
We belong to one another.
Let's tell everyone they're already in the Imago Dei.

7

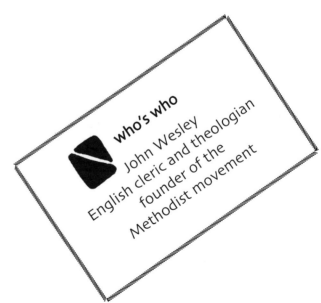
who's who
John Wesley
English cleric and theologian
founder of the
Methodist movement

week 7: bring
wednesday: servant leadership

 scripture

Isaiah 52:7–9

7 How beautiful upon the mountains
    are the feet of a messenger
    who proclaims peace,
    who brings good news,
    who proclaims salvation,
    who says to Zion, "Your God rules!"
8 Listen! Your lookouts lift their voice;
    they sing out together!
    Right before their eyes they see the Lord returning to Zion.
9 Break into song together, you ruins of Jerusalem!
The Lord has comforted his people and has redeemed Jerusalem.

 muévete

Devotional:

"God has entrusted us...with several talents...Such is the influence which we have over others, whether by their love and esteem of us, or by power; power to do them good or hurt, to help or hinder them in the circumstances of life. Add to these, that invaluable talent of time with which God entrusts us from moment to moment. Add, lastly, that on which all the rest depend, and without which they would all be curses, not blessings; namely, the grace of God, the power of his Holy Spirit, which alone works in us all that is acceptable in his sight."
– John Wesley (Sermon 51: The Good Steward)

How are you being invited to exercise your power and spend your time?

What is God inviting you to bring from this experience?

What is God inviting you to bring to the community today?

Jesus, Servant of the Lord, empower us in the gifts we bring. Equip us to lead from where we are.

week 7: bring
thursday: spiritual disciplines

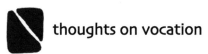 thoughts on vocation

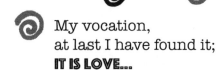

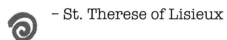

My vocation,
at last I have found it;
IT IS LOVE...
I understood that
love encompasses all vocations
and that **LOVE IS EVERYTHING.**
Love encompasses all times and places.

– St. Therese of Lisieux

liturgy of bringing

What do we carry from this place?
What have we gathered that needs to be shared?
Our lives, as Christ's, become an offering.
Our stories are ours, and they are also for the greater whole of the community.
We bring our collective wisdom and God-sightings to the table,
Together, we piece together a holy puzzle.
Reveal to us the justice that will emerge from our hands and feet,
Show us the opportunities to bring healing and hope with our words and our presence,
Teach us the story of Love and how to tell it.
Introduce us to one another again and again,
We belong to one another.
Let's tell everyone they're already in the Imago Dei.

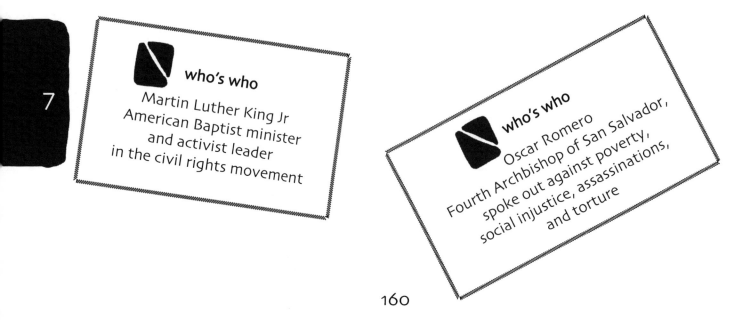

who's who
Martin Luther King Jr
American Baptist minister
and activist leader
in the civil rights movement

who's who
Oscar Romero
Fourth Archbishop of San Salvador,
spoke out against poverty,
social injustice, assassinations,
and torture

week 7: bring
thursday: spiritual disciplines

 **scripture**

1 John 4:12
No one has ever seen God. If we love each other, God remains in us and his love is made perfect in us.

What does it look, feel and sound like to love someone?

 **muévete**

Devotional:

"Let us not tire of preaching love. It is the force that will overcome the world."
– Oscar Romero

"Darkness cannot drive out darkness. Only light can do that.
Hatred cannot drive out hatred. Only love can do that."
– Martin Luther King Jr.

Preaching does not strictly mean "from the pulpit." How we live and breathe, how we respond and where we stand, these all point to that which we believe in; these can all tell a story. In a world often filled with the narratives of division, cruelty, fear, and violence, a narrative of love is revolutionary.

How can you practice a spiritual discipline of preaching love?

7

Imagine what this can look like in your context. Discuss it with a peer, house pastor, or staff member.

Spirit of the Living God, may this practice strengthen my spirit and equip me to dwell in your love.

week 7: bring
friday experience

 friday experience

before the friday experience

What are you feeling as you head towards this experience?

Expectations? Hopes? Concerns?

Why did you choose this particular Friday Experience?

What questions will you ask?

after the friday experience

What justice issues and healing gifts did you notice?

What surprised you about this Experience?

Did you feel energized or depleted while learning about this work?

How might you incorporate what you're learning when you go back home?

Is this a vocation that interests you?

weekend check-in

No judgment, just noticing. How are you listening to your soul this week?

I was present and fully engaged in muévete ☐

I practiced string prayer ☐

I did an intentional act of kindness ☐

I intentionally thought about my friday experience ☐

What do I want to remember from this week? (write it in this space)

7

week 7: bring
fifth day: Sabbath rest

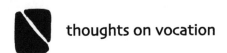 **thoughts on vocation**

> Many people
> mistake
> our work
> for our vocation.
> Our vocation
> is the
> love of Jesus.
>
> – Mother Teresa

 scripture

Psalm 126

1 When the Lord changed Zion's circumstances for the better,
   it was like we had been dreaming.
2 Our mouths were suddenly filled with laughter;
   our tongues were filled with joyful shouts.
It was even said, at that time, among the nations,
   "The Lord has done great things for them!"
3 Yes, the Lord has done great things for us,
   and we are overjoyed.
4 Lord, change our circumstances for the better,
   like dry streams in the desert waste!
5 Let those who plant with tears
   reap the harvest with joyful shouts.
6 Let those who go out,
   crying and carrying their seed,
   come home with joyful shouts,
   carrying bales of grain!

 muévete

Devotional:
What feels important to bring back home? (could be an experience, a discipline, a piece of wisdom, etc.)

What types of vocations or callings are resonating with you?

What does your soul need to enter into rest?

What are you praying for this week?

Good Shepherd, lead me into rest. Lead me beside still waters. On this day, restore my soul.

week 7: bring
journaling pages

7

7

7

7

7

Liturgy of Re-entry

We have done a good work, and the summer has done a good work within us.
The work is nearly completed. **We prepare to return.**
We have been changed and impacted by this time,
By being together,
By showing up.
Prepare us, Holy Guide, for the road ahead.
Lead us into spaces, relationships, and communities, where the work may continue.
Empower us to cultivate hope.
Empower us to tell a story of justice and compassion.
Empower us to sit in the hard places, and offer space to each other.
We are all in this journey together.

Prayers of the People

For the ways we have been changed, transformed, and challenged by this summer experience, and all that this means for our lives moving forward…
…God, guide our steps and our hearts as the learning and work continues.

For the relationships we have built, how they have sharpened us and we have sharpened them. We pray we have been good stewards of the dignity and humanity of others.
…God, strengthen our bonds so that we may continue to be seen, challenged, and shaped by this community and family we have created together.

For people we have not yet met, whose stories we have not yet heard, with whom we have not yet shared meals or tears. May you prepare us to be interrupted.
…Open our imagination to how you may arrive and bring others upon our path.

For the gifts we have discovered, the passions we have nurtured, the griefs we have held alongside one another.
…Give us the strength to keep standing in the gap between what is and what will be. Equip us to stay rooted so that we may continue the work of justice and healing in the world.

For your reign and power we have witnessed, may we continue to witness its in-breaking through-out our lives, in our work, in our homes, in our relationships, in our neighborhoods and community.
…Nurture us to be creative participants, co-working to bring about the reign of justice, peace, mercy, and love, on earth as it is in heaven. May we work for and see it in our homes, our families, our communities, our schools.

In your holy community of love, Creator, Son, and Holy Spirit, we pray, we participate, and we give thanks.

Amen.

week
8
re-entry

week 8: re-entry
living in balance

 mind

 imagination

 body

Your Project Transformation Journey began eight weeks ago. We started by looking at how to foster holistic health by focusing on Primary Foods:

- **Spiritual Practice**
- **Physical Activity**
- **Meaningful Work**
- **Relationships**

The intention behind each teaching and meditation exercise has been to strengthen those spiritual muscles, and, hopefully, provide tools for you to create change and spiritual growth in your own life.

Exercise Eight: Circle of Life (Take Two) Map your Circle of Life again.

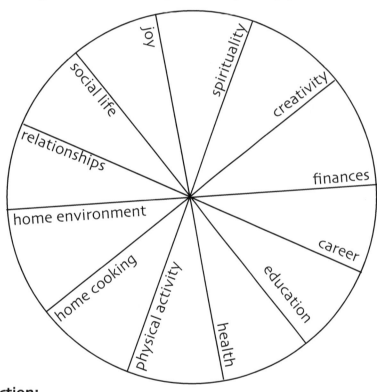

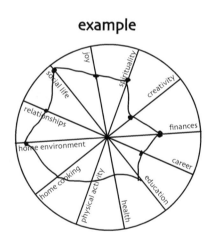

example

Reflection:

How does your Circle of Life differ from Week One?

Are there areas that have improved? If so, why?

Are there areas the appear stuck? If so, why?

What are some Top Ten steps you can take to create movement in those areas where satisfaction is low?

How will you use the framework of Primary Foods to shape your holistic health in the future?

Has looking at holistic health changed your perspective on spiritual practice and growth?

Will you continue any practices? If so, what?

week 8: re-entry
living in balance

 spirit

the practice of noticing

This **examen** can be useful in times of discernment (recognizing God's leading).

- Take a few moments to settle into a comfortable position with your journal. Let your muscles relax and your mind become quiet. Take a deep breath and know that you are in the presence of God and thank God for the gifts of the day.

- What decision is on your heart? A career choice, a change in relationship? Choose one for the focus of your examen prayer. It may help to frame your decision as a "yes or no" question.

- Think about the various factors involved in the decision. Ask God how these factors have affected your life in the recent past. Are you leaning in one direction? Has that leaning led to greater faith, hope, and love in your life?

- Make a list or chart of the decision's advantages and disadvantages to yourself—both for "yes" and for "no." After focusing on yourself, include others who may be affected by the decision.

- Choose a particular solution and sit with it as though the decision has been made. How does it feel? Consider your emotional response to the decision. Ask God to reveal any emotions you may have been neglecting regarding this decision. Are you moving toward God or away from God? Do you feel more peace as a result of making this decision or less? You may choose to then sit with the opposite decision and ask the same questions.

- If a friend came to you asking advice for the same decision for himself or herself, what advice would you give? Imagine yourself at the end of your life, looking back. Is there a direction you wish you had chosen?

- Ask God to help you respond to this prayer. You may or may not be ready to make the actual decision. Notice if this is a momentary leaning or if God has been nudging you for some time.

- Take a few minutes to write your reflections in the journaling pages. You may choose to talk with a trusted friend, mentor, pastor, teacher, spiritual director, or counselor about your experience and decision-making process.

8

week 8: re-entry
monday: identity formation

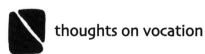 **thoughts on vocation**

One of the **biggest misconceptions** about vocation
is that the discovery of one's vocation is a **momentary happening**,
an **instant epiphany**, or a **lightning bolt** that illuminates the rest of our life's path.
The discovery of our vocation is, rather, a **process**, a **journey**.
There may be significant, discrete **moments of clarity** along the way,
but there is always **more to be discovered** and discerned.
On the vocational journey we never "arrive."
We are always "arriving."

– Renee LaReau

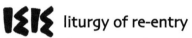 **liturgy of re-entry**

We have done a good work, and the summer has done a good work within us.

The work is nearly completed. **We prepare to return.**

We have been changed and impacted by this time,

By being together,

By showing up.

Prepare us, Holy Guide, for the road ahead.

Lead us into spaces, relationships, and communities, where the work may continue.

Empower us to cultivate hope.

Empower us to tell a story of justice and compassion.

Empower us to sit in the hard places, and offer space to each other.

We are all in this journey together.

8

who's who
Rainer Maria Rilke
Bohemian-Austrian poet
and novelist

monday: identity formation

 **scripture**

Psalm 27:13–14
13 But I have sure faith
   that I will experience the Lord's goodness
   in the land of the living!
14 Hope in the Lord!
   Be strong! Let your heart take courage!
      Hope in the Lord!

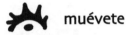 **muévete**

Devotional:
You have learned a great deal about yourself this summer.
What are you dreaming about as you prepare to head back home?

What anxieties do you feel?

"I beg you...to have patience
with everything unresolved in your heart
and try to love the questions themselves
As if they were locked rooms
Or books written in a very foreign language.
Don't search for the answers, which could not be given to you now,
Because you would not be able to live them.
And the point is
to live everything.
Live the questions now.
Perhaps then,
Someday far in the future,
You will gradually, without even noticing it,
Live your way into the answer..."
– Rainer Maria Rilke

What questions are working their way through you?

8

Creator God, whose image I bear, help me to pay attention to what is occurring within me.

 thoughts on vocation

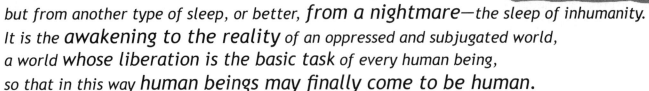

The fundamental change...consists of an **awakening,**
but from another type of sleep, or better, **from a nightmare**—*the sleep of inhumanity.*
It is the **awakening to the reality** *of an oppressed and subjugated world,*
a world **whose liberation is the basic task** *of every human being,*
so that in this way **human beings may finally come to be human.**

- Jon Sobrino

 muévete

Devotional:

"A new commandment I give to you, that you love one another
just as I have loved you, you also are to love one another.
By this all people will know that you are my disciples,
if you have love for one another."
— John 13:34–35

Take an opportunity to ask someone (a friend, house pastor, staff member, a child, or whomever you like) about their hopes and anxieties as the summer ends.

What is weighing on their heart and soul? What is exciting them about what's ahead?

Take in as many stories as you like from the people around you.

Community of Love, Parent, Son, and Holy Spirit, teach me to see your image in my brother, sister, enemy, friend, and neighbor.

8

week 8: re-entry
tuesday: intentional community

 scripture

John 13:34–35
"I give you a new commandment: Love each other. Just as I have loved you, so you also must love each other. 35 This is how everyone will know that you are my disciples, when you love each other."

1 John 4:7
"Dear friends, let's love each other, because love is from God, and everyone who loves is born from God and knows God."

 going deeper resource

Reading: Annie Dillard "Living Like Weasels"
Dillard muses upon the behavior of a weasel: Grab onto your life and calling and hold on tightly
http://m.dailygood.org/story/1490/living-like-weasels-annie-dillard/

Video: TED talk - Itay Talgam "Lead like the great conductors"
What can we learn about leadership from the orchestra conductor? Consider their wisdom in "creating perfect harmony without saying a word"

liturgy of re-entry

We have done a good work, and the summer has done a good work within us.

The work is nearly completed. **We prepare to return.**

We have been changed and impacted by this time,

By being together,

By showing up.

Prepare us, Holy Guide, for the road ahead.

Lead us into spaces, relationships, and communities, where the work may continue.

Empower us to cultivate hope.

Empower us to tell a story of justice and compassion.

Empower us to sit in the hard places, and offer space to each other.

We are all in this journey together.

8

 thoughts on vocation

> **VOCATION CONVEYS "CALLING."**
> **IT IS A RELATIONSHIP TO THE WHOLE OF LIFE.**
> **VOCATION ARISES FROM A DEEPENING UNDERSTANDING**
> **OF THE SUFFERING AND WONDER OF BOTH SELF AND WORLD—**
> **AND A SENSE THAT WHO YOU ARE IS IN SYNC**
> **WITH YOUR PLACE IN THE SCHEME OF THINGS,**
> **YOUR "CALLING," YOUR NICHE IN THE ECOLOGY OF LIFE.**
>
> **– SHARON DALOZ PARKS**

 muévete

Devotional:

Mary, as a humble, young, vulnerable woman, receives the invitation from the angel and says yes to birth and care for the child to be called Jesus. She clings to hope, and allows God's justice, mercy, and love to shape her vision of the world.

Our means of service and leadership do not have to be loud or filled with professional titles. Showing up to the needs and invitation of the moment can be enough.

When you think about where you are headed next through the lens of this summer experience, what needs and assets in your community are coming to mind?

How will you bring back methods of service and leadership from this experience?

Who models leadership and service well in the community there?

8

Jesus, Servant of the Lord, empower us in the gifts we bring. Equip us to lead from where we are.

week 8: re-entry
wednesday: servant leadership

 scripture

Luke 1:46–49, 52–55
46 Mary said,
"With all my heart I glorify the Lord!
47 In the depths of who I am I rejoice in God my savior.
48 He has looked with favor on the low status of his servant.
  Look! From now on, everyone will consider me highly favored
49 Holy is his name.

52 He has pulled the powerful down from their thrones
  and lifted up the lowly.
53 He has filled the hungry with good things
  and sent the rich away empty-handed.
54 He has come to the aid of his servant Israel,
  remembering his mercy,
55 just as he promised to our ancestors,
  to Abraham and to Abraham's descendants forever."

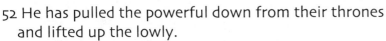 liturgy of re-entry
We have done a good work, and the summer has done a good work within us.
The work is nearly completed. **We prepare to return.**
We have been changed and impacted by this time,
By being together,
By showing up.
Prepare us, Holy Guide, for the road ahead.
Lead us into spaces, relationships, and communities, where the work may continue.
Empower us to cultivate hope.
Empower us to tell a story of justice and compassion.
Empower us to sit in the hard places, and offer space to each other.
We are all in this journey together.

 thoughts on vocation

Deep within us all, there is an amazing inner sanctuary of the soul, a holy place, a Divine Center, a speaking Voice, to which we may continuously return. Eternity is at our hearts, pressing upon our time-torn lives, warming us with intimations of an astounding destiny, calling us home unto itself.

- Thomas Kell

 muévete

Devotional:

"Imagination does significantly more than entertainment for children and its significance does not dissipate in the transition to adulthood. No organized sporting contest, no battle for liberation, no educational reform, no campaign for office, no quest for a corner office, no cry for release from captivity, no response to that cry, no charitable organization or humanitarian cause has ever been conceived or realized without the assistance of the imagination.
It is our window into the world that could be. In the case of the missional imagination, it is our window into the world that should be, can be and will be through the power of God."
– Bret Wells, leader and coach with the Missional Wisdom Foundation

Martin Luther King Jr. shared his dreams and imagination for a better tomorrow with the crowd at the Lincoln Memorial in 1963, and these words continue to inspire the imagination and work of others worldwide. What we imagine, we begin to speak. What we speak, we begin to live out. Together, this can change the world.

Invite yourself to imagine hope, justice, and compassion unfolding in the community and neighborhoods.
Imagine love and healing unfolding in your relationships and the economic and social systems around you.

How has imagination been practiced this summer?
How can you continue to practice the revolutionary act of imagination?

Spirit of the Living God, may this practice strengthen my spirit and equip me to dwell in your love.

8

week 8: re-entry
thursday: spiritual disciplines

 scripture

Ezekiel 37:1–3, 7–8, 10, 14

1 The Lord's power overcame me, and while I was in the Lord's spirit, he led me out and set me down in the middle of a certain valley. It was full of bones. 2 He led me through them all around, and I saw that there were a great many of them on the valley floor, and they were very dry.
3 He asked me, "Human one, can these bones live again?"
I said, "Lord God, only you know."

7 I prophesied just as I was commanded. There was a great noise as I was prophesying, then a great quaking, and the bones came together, bone by bone.8 When I looked, suddenly there were sinews on them. The flesh appeared, and then they were covered over with skin. But there was still no breath in them.

10 I prophesied just as he commanded me. When the breath entered them, they came to life and stood on their feet, an extraordinarily large company.

14 I will put my breath in you, and you will live. I will plant you on your fertile land, and you will know that I am the Lord. I've spoken, and I will do it. This is what the Lord says."

ИɛИɛ liturgy of re-entry

We have done a good work, and the summer has done a good work within us.
The work is nearly completed. **We prepare to return.**
We have been changed and impacted by this time,
By being together,
By showing up.
Prepare us, Holy Guide, for the road ahead.
Lead us into spaces, relationships, and communities, where the work may continue.
Empower us to cultivate hope.
Empower us to tell a story of justice and compassion.
Empower us to sit in the hard places, and offer space to each other.
We are all in this journey together.

8

week 8: re-entry
friday experience

 friday experience

before the friday experience

What are you feeling as you head towards this experience?

Expectations? Hopes? Concerns?

Why did you choose this particular Friday Experience?

What questions will you ask?

after the friday experience

What justice issues and healing gifts did you notice?

What surprised you about this Experience?

Did you feel energized or depleted while learning about this work?

How might you incorporate what you're learning when you go back home?

Is this a vocation that interests you?

weekend check-in

No judgment, just noticing. How are you listening to your soul this week?

I was present and fully engaged in muévete ☐

I practiced examen for discernment ☐

I charted my Wheel of Life ☐

I intentionally thought about my friday experience ☐

8

What do I want to remember from this week? (write it in this space)

thoughts on vocation

Oh God, I thank you for having created me as I am. I thank you for the sense of fulfillment I sometimes have: that fulfillment is after all nothing but being filled with You. I promise You to strive my whole life long for beauty and harmony and also humility and true love, whispers of which I hear inside me during my best moments.
– Etty Hillesum

 scripture

Isaiah 52:7
How beautiful upon the mountains are the feet of a messenger who proclaims peace, who brings good news, who proclaims salvation, who says to Zion, "Your God rules!"

ᛁᚦᛁᚦ liturgy of re-entry

We have done a good work, and the summer has done a good work within us.
The work is nearly completed. **We prepare to return.**
We have been changed and impacted by this time,
By being together,
By showing up.
Prepare us, Holy Guide, for the road ahead.
Lead us into spaces, relationships, and communities, where the work may continue.
Empower us to cultivate hope.
Empower us to tell a story of justice and compassion.
Empower us to sit in the hard places, and offer space to each other.
We are all in this journey together.

 muévete

Devotional:
What will be important to remember as you re-enter your home life?

What types of vocations or callings are resonating with you?

What does your soul need to enter into rest?

What are you praying for this week?

Good Shepherd, lead me into rest. Lead me beside still waters. On this day, restore my soul.

8

8

8

8

8

week 8: re-entry
journaling pages

8

188

8

 going deeper resource

Scribble Prayer

For this prayer, first, turn off the analytical part of the brain so that the intuitive side can play. After play, it is also important to then allow the analytical part to join in and think about what just happened. We need both. Art is wonderful, but it is the thinking and asking God to help understand our feelings and images in the art that makes the process of art-making into a spiritual practice. Sometimes when we pray if feels like talking at God; in this prayer we are listening for God. Make space.

Instructions:

Turn to one of the blank unlined pages in the journaling pages of this guidebook. You will also need a pencil with eraser and some kind of coloring medium: colored pencils, markers, crayons, etc. Once you have gathered your supplies, take a few moments to focus on your breathing and to settle your mind. Open your spirit to listen to God the Creator. Choose a focus for your prayer: it could be a situation, a person, or "Who am I?" Once that focus comes to mind, simply repeat it in your mind a few times. Leave room for God to speak.

Close your eyes and use your non-dominant hand to scribble out whatever feels right on the page (your scribble may take up the whole page or be more confined—follow your intuition). When it feels finished, open your eyes and look at the scribble. Turn the page sideways, upside down, looking at the scribble from each angle until an image appears in the scribble. What do you see? If there are images in more than one viewpoint, choose the strongest one (the one that "feels" the most).

Using your colors (crayons, pencils, watercolors), fill out the image. You may add anything you like to the scribble and you may erase the extra lines from the scribble (the scribble is only intended to give you a starting point for your picture). Allow your intuition to play and make the picture complete, whatever that is for you.

When the picture feels finished, take at least twenty minutes to sit and look at it, thinking about your picture. Write about this process and the image you made in the journaling pages. How did it come to be? How do you feel about that? How does this image connect to what's going on in your life? Do you see yourself here? Someone else? What kind of environment is it? If one color dominates the scene, does that color mean something specific to you? What is the Spirit revealing to you?

next
steps
being

after returning home
living in balance

next steps and future plans

"If you are depressed, you are living in the past.
If you are anxious, you are living in the future.
If you are at peace, you are living in the present."
Lao Tzu, "Tao Te Ching"

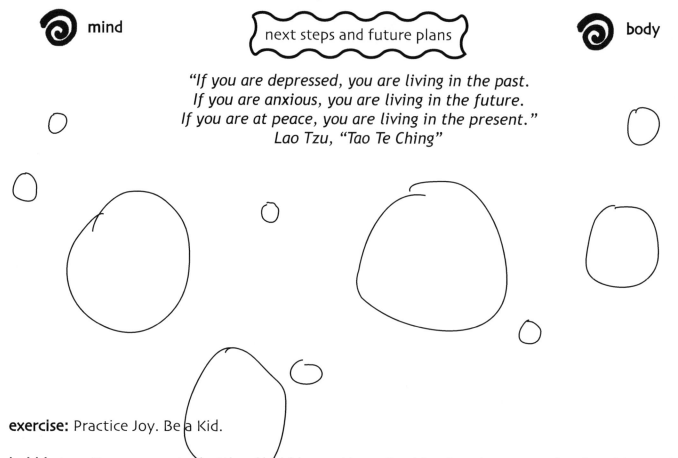

exercise: Practice Joy. Be a Kid.

bubble tag: Everyone get a bottle of bubbles and have fun blowing them at each other, like you're playing tag. Make sure you're laughing and doing whatever silly thing comes into your mind. The only rule is to blow bubbles at each other. You can make up more rules.

Take time to blow some bubbles and watch how magical they are. Remember the simple joy of being a child. Keep remembering childlike joy, and keep blowing bubbles.

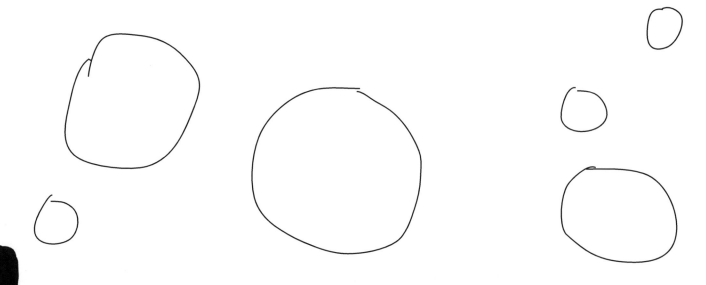

P

after returning home
living in balance

 spirit

the practice of dedicating space

You have been given some ideas and tools, which hopefully have sparked new avenues for prayer and spiritual growth. This final section is designed to help you take these practices home and continue to nurture your spirit. You may have enjoyed some of the practices in this book, you may not. Learning what nourishes your spirit is an important piece of spiritual development. As you move back into life, continue to learn about and practice various kinds of prayer. Keep those that help you feel closer to God; dismiss prayer forms that you don't find to be life-giving.

Pray as you can, not as you can't.

create a prayer box
The items you choose to put in this box will be just for your prayer time. Decorate the box if you like and collect things you can see, touch, smell, hear, and taste to keep in the box. Consider including pictures, a candle, or water; music to inspire you; a piece of soft blanket; or an item from nature. Use objects that have personal meaning for you and tell the story of your spiritual journey.

In your prayer time, light your candle, settle your mind, and breathe for a few moments. Look at the items you have gathered. Choose one that seems to be calling to you most strongly, and hold it in your hand. Feel its surface. Notice how you feel when you are holding that item.

Spend time with the item for the prayer, asking God why you chose that particular item in this moment: is there something that feels like this going on in your life? In your spirit? Is God asking you to respond in some way?

End with a prayer of thanks for each special object in your prayer space.

start a circle
In your spiritual journey, be intentional about developing spiritual relationships and listening skills. If you enjoy praying with others, you may intentionally commit to being a prayer partner or form a prayer circle and meet regularly to pray.

Basic circle rules:
   allow everyone an opportunity to speak or not speak as they are comfortable, answering the question: "How is it with your soul?"
- set a time limit and use a timer to ensure equal talking time for everyone; consider using a talking piece (a person only talks when holding the talking piece)

- speakers talk only of their own self and specific experience using "I" statements (such as "I felt..." or "I realized..."). Avoid complaining, finger-pointing, and generalizations

- listeners say nothing but "thank you for sharing" (no giving advice, fixing, or helping)

optional meditation: after everyone answers the "how is it with your soul?" question, sit together in silent meditation for fifteen or twenty minutes.

P

after returning home
being

 liturgy of being

God may you send us
To the places we need go
We have been changed
And imbued with capacity to change
Equip us with your Spirit
To be
who and where we need be
For the sake of healing
Justice
And mercy
Ambassadors of kin-dom
Throughout the world

Nurture in us compassion
For each
Other
And ourselves
Mold us in mercy
Make us in grace
Move us in love
So that we might join with your presence
Hovering over waters of chaos
Creative and collaborative
Peace-making wherever your Spirit takes us

thoughts on vocation

[A womanist biblical scholar]
must **constantly**
make **available** *to God*
her **fallible** *humanity*
so that God might **continually**
encourage, transform, and
regenerate *her for the* **work**
she is called to do
for herself
and her **community.**

- Mitzi J. Smith

who's who
Mitzi J. Smith
author of
I Found God in Me: A Womanist
Biblical Hermeneutics Reader

Did I offer peace today?
Did I bring a smile to someone's face?
Did I say words of healing?
Did I let go of my anger and resentment?
Did I forgive?
Did I love?

These are the real questions.

I must trust that the little bit of love
that I sow now will bear many fruits,
here in this world and the life to come.

- Henri Nouwen

"I will bless you...and
all the families of the earth
will be blessed because of you."

- God; Genesis 12:2, 3

P

after returning home
being

 scripture

John 17:18–25

"As you sent me into the world, so I have sent them into the world. I made myself holy on their behalf so that they also would be made holy in the truth. "I'm not praying only for them but also for those who believe in me because of their word. I pray they will be one, Father, just as you are in me and I am in you. I pray that they also will be in us, so that the world will believe that you sent me. I've given them the glory that you gave me so that they can be one just as we are one. I'm in them and you are in me so that they will be made perfectly one. Then the world will know that you sent me and that you have loved them just as you loved me. "Father, I want those you gave me to be with me where I am. Then they can see my glory, which you gave me because you loved me before the creation of the world. "Righteous Father, even the world didn't know you, but I've known you, and these believers know that you sent me.

 muévete

The work of this summer has been done and accomplished. The way ahead will be shaped by how you arrive. What has been born in you in the work and community of this summer?

Go forth. Encounter God in the practices, postures, and presence you've nurtured here. Continue to arrive: to the Spirit of God who always rises to greet you, to the community of Christ ever called to walk together, and to the road and this day that beckons you forward.

Creator God, who art in the heavens all around us, holy is your way of being. Thy kin-dom and way of togetherness and community, come; enable us to do as you would do in love, compassion, grace, and justice, in this earthly life as it is in the heavenly presence among us. Give us today that which we need, and invite us to step into release and forgiveness for all that we've done to cause injury, for all the ways we've devalued the life within and surrounding us. Empower us to release others unto themselves and into you; help us embrace that we are all doing the best we can in our messy humanity together. Allow us to embrace forgiveness from the earth and nature around us, help us to be better stewards of all the life surrounding us, in whose presence we humbly stand. Deliver and guide us away from that which harms us; that which allows us to participate in systems and actions that harm. Make us in your image: creative, redeeming, advocating, healing presence, that this world and all its life might be loved and honored by our presence. Amen.

P

after returning home
journaling pages

P

P

P

after returning home
journaling pages

P

P

P

bibliography

bibliography

 muévete

week 1: open
Ajayi, Luvvie. "Get Comfortable with Being Uncomfortable." Filmed November 2017 at TEDWom-
    en2017. TED video. 10:55. https://www.ted.com/talks/luvvie_ajayi_get_comfortable_with_be-
    ing_uncomfortable.

week 2: brokenness
Doyle, Glennon. "Glennon Doyle Melton at Together Rising Atlanta." Filmed October 19, 2016 in Atlan-
    ta, GA. YouTube video, 1:44. https://www.youtube.com/watch?v=O8OfaFRQ3sI.

Haque, Umair. "How to Have a Year That Matters." Harvard Business Review. January 22, 2013.
    https://hbr.org/2013/01/how-to-have-a-year-that-matter.

Neighboring Movement, "About Us." NeighboringMovement.Org by SoCe Life. (Accessed March 2,
    2018).http://neighboringmovement.org/aboutus/.

Cain, Susan. Quiet: The Power of Introverts in a World that Can't Stop Talking. Crown/Archetype, 2012.

Parker Palmer, "The Broken-Open Heart." This is an excerpt by author/educator Parker J. Palmer from
    Weavings: A Journal of the Christian Spiritual Life, March/April 2009, Vol. XXIV, No. 2. Copy-
    right 2008 by Upper Room Ministries® , Nashville, TN. Art used with permission of the artist.
    All rights reserved. Learn more at www.couragerenewal.org." © Center for Courage & Renewal,
    founded by Parker J. Palmer. https://www.couragerenewal.org/PDFs/PJP-WeavingsArticle-Bro-
    ken-OpenHeart.pdf

week 3: show up
Nash, Marilyn. "Keeping Vigil With Wisdom." Ignatian Solidarity Network blog. November 13, 2017.
    https://ignatiansolidarity.net/blog/2017/11/13/keeping-vigil-wisdom/

Watson, Lilla. "The Origin of 'Our Liberty is Bound Together'." Invisible Children website. Accessed
    March 2, 2018. https://invisiblechildren.com/blog/2012/04/04/the-origin-of-our-liberty-is-
    bound-together/

week 4: listen
Cone, James. God of the Oppressed. New York: Orbis Books, 1997.

Lacz, Katie. "Do Not Be Afraid - There Is Good News." Ignatian Spirituality Network blog. December
    25, 2017. https://ignatiansolidarity.net/blog/2017/12/25/do-not-be-afraid-there-is-good-news/

Palmer, Parker. "The Tragic Gap." Center for Courage and Renewal website. Accessed March 2, 2018.
    http://www.couragerenewal.org/the-tragic-gap/

bibliography

 muévete

week 5: presence

Yousafzai, Malala. I am Malala: The Girl Who Stood Up For Education and Was Shot By the Taliban. New York: Back Bay Books, 2015.

Palmer, Parker. "The Gift of Presence, The Perils of Advice." OnBeing website. April 27, 2016. https://onbeing.org/blog/the-gift-of-presence-the-perils-of-advice/.

Smith, Clint. "The Danger of Silence." Filmed July 2014 at TED@NYC video in New York, NY. 4:19. https://www.ted.com/talks/clint_smith_the_danger_of_silence.

week 6: release

Lynn Ungar, Camas Lilies. This poem appears in her book, Bread and Other Miracles, and her website www.lynnungar.com. Used with permission.

Linn, Dennis, Sheila Fabricant Linn, and Matthew Linn. Sleeping with Bread: Holding What Gives You Life. Mahwah, New Jersey: Paulist Press, 1995.

Su'ad Abdul Khabeer (@DrSuad), "You don't need to be a voice for the voiceless. Just pass the mic," Twitter, February 12, 2017, 10:00 am, https://twitter.com/drsuad/status/830838928403988480?lang=en.

week 7: bring

Harris-Perry, Melissa. Sister Citizen: Shame, Stereotypes, and Black Women in America. Yale University Press, 2011.

Henderson, Wesley. Under Whose Shade: A Story of a Pioneer in the Swan River Valley of Manitoba. Nepean, Ontario, Canada: Wes Henderson & Associates, Incorporated, 1986.

Flippin Jr., Rev. William E. "Ubuntu: Applying African Philosophy in Building Community." HuffPost Blog. April 6, 2012.

Black Panther. Film. Directed by Ryan Coogler. Released February 16, 2018.

https://www.huffingtonpost.com/reverend-william-e-flippin-jr/ubuntu-applying-african-p_b_1243904.html.

Outler, Albert C. and Richard P. Heitzenrater, eds. John Wesley's Sermons: An Anthology. Abingdon Press: 1991.

week 8: re-entry

Rilke, Rainer Maria. Letters to a Young Poet. BN Publishing, 2008.

bibliography

⬡⬡⬡⬡⬡⬡⬡⬡⬡ going deeper resources

Winch, Guy, "Why we all need to practice emotional first aid," Filmed November 2014 at TEDxLinnae-usUniversity, TED video, 17:24, https://www.ted.com/talks/guy_winch_the_case_for_emotional_hygiene?language=en

Ajayi, Luvvie. "Get Comfortable with Being Uncomfortable." Filmed November 2017 at TEDWomen2017. TED video. 10:55. https://www.ted.com/talks/luvvie_ajayi_get_comfortable_with_being_uncomfortable.

Parker Palmer, "The Broken-Open Heart." This is an excerpt by author/educator Parker J. Palmer from Weavings: A Journal of the Christian Spiritual Life, March/April 2009, Vol. XXIV, No. 2. Copyright 2008 by Upper Room Ministries® , Nashville, TN. Art used with permission of the artist. All rights reserved. Learn more at www.couragerenewal.org." © Center for Courage & Renewal, founded by Parker J. Palmer. https://www.couragerenewal.org/PDFs/PJP-WeavingsArticle-Broken-OpenHeart.pdf

Brown, Brene, "The power of vulnerability," Filmed June 2010 at TEDxHouston, TED video, 20:13, https://www.ted.com/talks/brene_brown_on_vulnerability?language=en

Elizabeth Cady Stanton, ""Solitude of Self," Address before the Committee of the Judiciary of the United States Congress, January 18, 1892," Civil Rights and Conflict in the United States: Selected Speeches, Lit2Go Edition, (1892), accessed March 12, 2018, http://etc.usf.edu/lit2go/185/civil-rights-and-conflict-in-the-united-states-selected-speeches/4854/solitude-of-self-address-before-the-committee-of-the-judiciary-of-the-united-states-congress-january-18-1892/.

Wade, Cleo. "Want to change the world? Start by being brave enough to care." Filmed November 2017 at TEDWomen 2017. TED video, 11:01. https://www.ted.com/talks/cleo_wade_want_to_change_the_world_start_by_being_brave_enough_to _care.

Tan, Amy. Two Kinds. YouTube video. Narrated by Barbara Manrique. https://youtu.be/YhT4soKCzNk.

Stirolli, Ernest, "Want to help someone? Shut up and listen!" Filmed September 2012 at TEDxEQChCh, TED video, 17:03, https://www.ted.com/talks/ernesto_sirolli_want_to_help_someone_shut_up_and_listen?language=en

Palmer, Parker. "The Gift of Presence, The Perils of Advice." OnBeing website. April 27, 2016. https://onbeing.org/blog/the-gift-of-presence-the-perils-of-advice/.

Albani, Chris, "On Humanity," FIlmed in February 2008 at TED2008, TED video, 16:05, https://www.ted.com/talks/chris_abani_muses_on_humanity?language=en

bibliography

Adichie, Chimamanda Ngozi. "The Danger of a Single Story." Filmed July 2009 at TEDGlobal2009. TED video, 18:49. https://www.ted.com/talks/chimamanda_adichie_the_danger_of_a_single_ story/transcript.

Wapnick, Emilie. "Why some of us don't have a true calling." Filmed October 2015 at TEDxBend. TED video, 12:27. https://www.ted.com/talks/emilie_wapnick_why_some_of_us_don_t_have_one_ true_calling.

Dillard, Annie. "Living Like Weasels." DailyGood.org. May 25, 2017. http://m.dailygood.org/sto-ry/1490/living-like-weasels-annie-dillard/.
cessed March 1, 2018)

Talgam, Itay, "Lead like the great conductors," FIlmed July 2009 at TEDGlobal 2009, TED video, 20:45, https://www.ted.com/talks/itay_talgam_lead_like_the_great_conductors?language=en

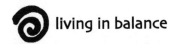 **table liturgy**

Delistraty, Cody C. "The Importance of Eating Together." The Atlantic, July 18, 2014. https://www. theatlantic.com/health/archive/2014/07/the-importance-of-eating-together/374256/ (Accessed March 1, 2018).

living in balance

week 2
Cameron, Julia. *The Artist's Way: A Spiritual Path to Higher Creativity.* New York: TarcherPerigree, 1992.

Reimagining Examen (app)

week 3
Sybil MacBeth - Praying in Color
www.prayingincolor.com

week 6
scribble prayer color charts
www.empower-yourself-with-color-psychology.com

week 8
modified pantoum poem
www.poets.org/poetsorg/text/pantoum-poetic-form

Made in United States
Orlando, FL
25 April 2024